YOUR RETIREMENT BLIND SPOT™

SMART STRATEGIES FOR NAVIGATING THE PERSONAL AND FINANCIAL CONSEQUENCES OF LONG-TERM CARE

ZACH OTT, CLTC®

IMPORTANT NOTICE

ISBN: 979-8-9959517-0-4 Paperback
ISBN: 979-8-9959517-1-1 E-book
Library of Congress Control Number: 2026911666

First Edition, 2026
Printed in the United States of America

WWW.YOURRETIREMENTBLINDSPOT.COM

*"It is better to have a map
and not need it, than to need
a map and not have it."*

ANCIENT EXPLORER'S MAXIM

For our mother, Pamela
You cheered our every step. We stood with
you for your last one. Our inspiration always.
We love you and miss you dearly.
Forever your sons, Zach and Justin

READERS' BONUS

To download free practical tools and resources
to help you navigate more easily, visit:

WWW.YOURRETIREMENTBLINDSPOT.COM/RESOURCES

INTRODUCTION

Most of us picture our later years filled with travel, family gatherings, and the freedom to enjoy what we've worked so hard to achieve.

But for millions of Americans, the reality of aging looks different: a gradual change in health, a diagnosis that alters daily routines, or the slow realization that simple tasks, like managing medications or preparing meals, aren't as easy as they once were.

These moments rarely arrive with warning. They unfold quietly, sometimes over months or years. And when they do, they don't just affect you. They can ripple through your entire family.

The Hidden Crisis in Retirement Planning

Living longer is one of modern life's greatest gifts. But it comes with a sobering reality: Whether it's due to a disability, a chronic illness, or other health challenges, a person turning 65 today has a nearly 70% chance of needing long-term care services and support in the years they have left.[1]

Women live an average of six years longer than men,[2] which means they should plan for more years of long-term care.

Despite the overwhelming likelihood of needing long-term care services, also known as extended care, only a small fraction of Americans are adequately prepared. As of 2020, just 7.5 million people had long-term care insurance,[3] which translates to approximately one in forty-four Americans, in a population exceeding 330 million.[4]

This staggering gap means that when long-term care needs arise, the vast majority of families find themselves scrambling without a formal plan, desperately hoping that personal savings will stretch far enough, that family members can shoulder the burden indefinitely, or that government programs will somehow fill the void.

Why do so many people overlook this risk? Often, it's because of common assumptions, such as:

- Thinking the need for care is unlikely, or something to worry about later

- Thinking there is a higher probability of it happening to others more than themselves

- Trusting that family will be able to step in if needed

- Hoping their retirement savings will be sufficient, yet not knowing the severity or duration of a potential long-term care need they might face

- Believing Medicare or health insurance will help cover long-term care needs and expenses

A Growing National Challenge

This isn't just a personal issue. It's a national challenge. As America's demographic landscape shifts toward an older population, experts warn of significant consequences that could overwhelm families, strain the healthcare system, and put unprecedented pressure on our economy.

By 2030, all Baby Boomers will be age 65 or older. The number of seniors needing long-term services and supports is expected to more than double, rising from 6.3 million in 2015 to an estimated 15 million by 2050.[5][6]

The "care gap" is widening as fewer family members are available to provide care. Without proper planning, the strain on families and the nation could reach epidemic proportions.

A Personal Wake-Up Call

I learned firsthand what millions of families discover every year: long-term care doesn't announce itself. When my mother was diagnosed with stage four cancer, my brother and I were instantly transformed from children into caregivers, desperately trying to hold our own lives together while ensuring she received the care and dignity she deserved.

Even though our time as caregivers lasted only months, it left scars that will never fully heal, and a sobering awareness that millions of families endure this same torment for years, watching their loved ones decline while their own lives crumble around them.

The devastation is far-reaching, emotionally, physically, and financially. Dreams of a comfortable retirement vanish. Life savings disappear faster than anyone imagined possible. Siblings who once celebrated holidays together now battle over care decisions and money.

That brutal awakening compelled me to write this book, to spare other families the agony of facing this crisis without a plan.

The Hidden Risk in Your Retirement Plan

Consider this: You've saved and invested diligently, built a comfortable monthly retirement income, and feel secure. But if long-term care needs arise, bringing significant new expenses, your plans could quickly be disrupted. It's a scenario that catches many families off guard, and it's more common than most people realize. This isn't speculation. It's a reality many families face.

There's a Better Way

The good news? With proper planning, you can protect everything you've worked for. This book shows you how. Not through wishful thinking or "self-insuring" (which is just assuming 100% of the risk as there is no actual insurance involved), but through proven strategies that preserve your independence and protect your loved ones.

But before we dive into strategies and solutions, I need you to pause and consider three fundamental questions.

1. **The Longevity Reality:** Is it a possibility you could live into your later decades? Artificial intelligence is transforming healthcare, from early disease detection to personalized treatment protocols, while healthier lifestyles add years to our lives. Together, these forces mean many of us will live well into our 80s, 90s, or beyond. If you can acknowledge this possibility, we continue.

2. **The Care Probability:** If you do enjoy those extra years, do you recognize that living longer often means facing health challenges that require extended care, and that without a plan, you risk becoming a caregiving or financial burden on those you love most? The statistics we've already discussed make this more than possible. It's probable. If you can acknowledge this reality, we're aligned.

3. **The Planning Imperative:** Do you understand that a formal, documented strategy for accessing and funding care isn't optional, it's essential for protecting both yourself and your family? Planning isn't pessimism. It's protection. It's the difference between maintaining control and losing it when you're most vulnerable.

If you cannot honestly agree with these three realities, if you believe you'll never need care, or that "something will work out," or that your family will simply figure it out when the time comes, then I respectfully suggest you may not be ready for this conversation. At least not yet.

But if these questions resonate with you, if you're ready to confront these possibilities and take meaningful action, then this book will provide you with the framework, tools, and insights to create a comprehensive plan that preserves your dignity, protects your assets, and shields your loved ones from the devastating consequences of unplanned care. Let's begin.

What You'll Discover

This book will guide you through the essential concepts, decisions, and actions that make up a personalized and thorough long-term care plan. The book is structured in the following sections:

1. **Understanding Long-Term Care:** Long-term care touches almost every family, but few understand what it really means, or how it impacts both personal and financial well-being. This section explains what it is and why advance planning is essential regardless of your wealth or health status.

2. **Paying for Long-Term Care:** Many people assume health insurance, Medicare, or savings will be enough to cover care, but the reality is very different. This section explains the true costs and explores smart funding solutions that protect both your assets and your independence.

3. **Creating Your Long-Term Care Plan:** An effective plan balances personal preferences, financial resources, and legal protections. This section shows how to assess your needs, structure your plan, and make sure your legal documents actually work when they're needed most.

4. **Special Planning Situations:** Long-term care planning differs for everyone. This section addresses special considerations for couples, singles, business owners, and those coordinating care with broader financial planning.

5. **Taking Action:** A plan only works if it's acted on. This section helps you take the right steps, communicate with your family, work with professionals, and update your plan as life changes.

6. **Tools & Resources:** This section provides access to worksheets, comparison tools, and checklists to help turn planning into action.

HOW TO GET THE MOST OUT OF THIS BOOK

Consider this book your all-encompassing guide and navigational tool for the complex terrain of long-term care planning.

Long-term care planning involves decisions that touch on every aspect of your life—your finances, your family, and your deepest values.

It can feel overwhelming, which is why this book is designed to provide clarity, direction, and actionable steps. No matter where you are in your planning process, you'll find the guidance you need here.

Finding Your Path

This book is organized to serve different needs. While it is designed to be read sequentially, you can also navigate it based on your most pressing questions.

- **For the Strategic Planner:** If you are building your first plan, start at the beginning. Each section builds on the last, creating a comprehensive understanding that moves from foundational knowledge to a personalized, actionable plan.

- **For the Financial Decision-Maker:** If your primary concern is the financial architecture of a plan, begin with Section 3 to explore funding strategies. Then, proceed to Section 4 to see how these strategies integrate with your broader retirement and estate plan.

- **For the Experienced Caregiver:** If you are currently providing care for a loved one, or have in the past, you know what most people can't imagine: the exhaustion, the emotional weight, the financial strain, and the life you've put on hold. You've seen what happens when there's no plan. That experience gives you clarity. You know exactly what you don't want your own family to endure. Use these pages to translate what you've learned into a plan that spares them from the same burden. The strategies you wish had been in place for your loved one can become the foundation of protection for yourself. Your experience is your roadmap to ensuring your family doesn't face the same reality.

The Tools Inside

Throughout the book, you'll find features designed to help you understand, navigate, and act:

- **Chapter at a Glance:** Key concepts summarized at the beginning of each chapter so you can quickly grasp the core ideas.

- **Key Points:** Critical insights and foundational principles that anchor each section's discussion.

- **Bottom Line Boxes:** Concise summaries of crucial points, allowing you to capture essential information at a glance.

- **Navigator Stories:** Real-world hypothetical examples illustrating how the principles in this book apply to families just like yours.

- **Action Steps:** Specific, concrete tasks at the end of each chapter that build progressively to create your comprehensive long-term care plan.

Making This Book Your Own

The fact that you've picked up this book (and made it this far) tells me you've already done what most people won't: you've confronted the longevity reality, acknowledged the care probability, and accepted that planning isn't optional.

Whether it's a personal caregiving experience that brought you here, the fear of burdening your family, or the worry about running out of money and losing control, you're seeking the knowledge to make informed choices that protect your family, preserve your assets, and maintain your dignity. That's exactly what this resource provides.

As you work through these pages, you'll find spaces for notes and reflections. Some readers prefer to highlight key passages, others like to jot thoughts in the margins. The goal is to make this book work for your learning style.

The time you invest in engaging with this material will pay dividends in the form of a plan that provides profound peace of mind.

When You Feel Overwhelmed

It is normal to feel stuck or resistant at various points in this process. When this happens, take a breath and remember that any planning is better than no planning.

Return to a previous chapter, complete one small action step, or simply discuss what you're learning with someone you trust. Progress, not perfection, is the goal.

Final Word Before You Begin

The best time to plan for long-term care was ten years ago. The second-best time is today.

There's no one-size-fits-all solution to long-term care planning. Your financial situation, family dynamics, health history, and personal values all play a role in determining what makes sense for you.

This book's purpose is not to tell you what to do. It's a tool to help you understand the landscape so you can navigate it on your own terms. Some readers will discover insurance solutions that feel right for their situation. Others will find different approaches that better suit their needs.

What long-term care planning looks like for your unique situation starts on the next page. The choice, as always, remains yours.

UNDERSTANDING LONG-TERM CARE

Long-term care will touch most families, yet few are prepared for its personal and financial impact.

This section clarifies what long-term care means today, why nearly everyone is at risk, and why advance planning is essential.

By facing these realities now, you can build a strategy that protects your assets and your family—no matter your current health or wealth.

WHAT IS LONG-TERM CARE?

- *Long-term care covers a range of services beyond just nursing homes*

- *The majority of long-term care in the U.S. is provided at home by unpaid family members and friends* [7]

- *Up to 70% of Americans turning 65 will need some long-term care* [8]

- *Care needs differ by gender: women average 3.7 years, men 2.2 years* [9]

- *Long-term care isn't just for the elderly – 37% of adult day services center participants are under age 65* [10]

BEYOND THE NURSING HOME: UNDERSTANDING TODAY'S LONG-TERM CARE

Long-term care encompasses a range of services designed to meet health and personal care needs over an extended period.

It differs from acute medical care, which focuses on treating specific illnesses or injuries.

Long-term care addresses the basic activities of daily living that many take for granted until they become challenging.

Throughout this book, long-term care (sometimes referred to as extended care or LTC) means help with activities of daily living or supervision due to cognitive impairment, provided at home, in assisted living, or in nursing facilities. It is distinct from Medicare's short-term 'skilled nursing facility' rehabilitation.

Most long-term care is actually custodial care, non-medical assistance with daily activities that can be provided by non-licensed caregivers. Unlike skilled care, which requires licensed health professionals following a physician's orders, custodial care focuses on helping with everyday tasks and ensuring safety. This distinction is crucial because Medicare generally does not cover custodial care, though it may cover limited skilled care.

At its core, long-term care supports individuals who struggle with activities of daily living (ADLs) such as transferring (moving from bed to chair), toileting, bathing, dressing, eating, and maintaining continence.

It may also assist with instrumental activities of daily living (IADLs) like managing medications, preparing meals, housekeeping, managing finances, and transportation.

The need for extended care can arise from various circumstances, such as:

- Aging-related frailty
- Cognitive conditions like Alzheimer's disease
- Chronic illnesses such as Parkinson's or multiple sclerosis
- Disabilities resulting from accidents or injuries

Regardless of the cause, the goal remains consistent: to help individuals maintain dignity, safety, and the highest possible quality of life when they can no longer independently manage daily activities.

Perhaps the most persistent misconception about extended care is that it refers exclusively to nursing home care. This outdated view fails to recognize the diverse, evolving landscape of care options available today.

BOTTOM LINE: Long-term care isn't just about nursing homes. It's a spectrum of services that help people maintain dignity and quality of life when they can no longer independently manage daily activities due to physical or cognitive limitations. Most commonly, this means custodial care—everyday assistance that helps people safely navigate their daily routines when they can no longer do so independently.

THE CARE CONTINUUM: FROM HOME TO SPECIALIZED COMMUNITIES

Long-term care exists on a spectrum, adapting to an individual's changing needs and preferences. Understanding this continuum helps clarify the range of options available when planning for potential care needs.

The key elements in this continuum are as follows:

Home Care: The Foundation of Long-Term Care

Home care represents the least restrictive option, allowing people to receive assistance while remaining in the familiar comfort of their own homes.

Services range from a few hours of help with household chores to round-the-clock skilled nursing care.

If you're like most Americans, you want to stay in your own home as long as possible. According to AARP in 2021, if given the choice, 77% of adults over 50 would prefer to age in place.[11]

Home care can be provided by family members (informal care) or by professional caregivers (formal care). Both typically provide custodial care, assistance with daily activities and supervision, though formal care may also include skilled medical services when needed.

Professional home care typically falls into two categories: homemaker services (meal preparation, light housekeeping, errands) and personal care services (assistance with bathing, dressing, and other ADLs).

More specialized services, such as skilled nursing or physical therapy, may also be provided at home when medically necessary.

The flexibility of home care allows it to be tailored to individual needs and preferences.

Care can be scheduled for a few hours weekly or provided around the clock, depending on the level of assistance required.

This adaptability makes home care suitable for a wide range of situations, from early-stage needs to more advanced care requirements when supported by appropriate resources.

Adult Day Care: Community Support with Home Living

Adult day care provides supervision, socialization, and structured activities during daytime hours while allowing individuals to return home in the evenings.

This option often serves as a respite for family caregivers who work during the day or need regular breaks from caregiving responsibilities. Most adult day care centers operate during business hours, Monday through Friday, though some offer weekend or evening services.

They typically provide social interaction, meals, recreational activities and varying levels of health services.

Some centers specialize in dementia care, offering programs specifically designed for those with cognitive impairments.

Adult day care represents an important middle option that supports both care recipients and family caregivers.

It provides meaningful engagement and supervision for those needing care while allowing family caregivers to maintain employment or attend to other responsibilities.

Board and Care Homes: A Home-Like Environment

Board and care homes are smaller facilities, often resembling private houses, that offer a home-like environment for small groups of elderly residents.

Residents may have their own rooms but typically share dining areas with other group home members.

Staff members provide help with personal care and the activities of daily living intermittently throughout the day; however, they do not provide medical or nursing care.

These facilities are also referred to as "group homes" and typically do not offer planned activities or transportation services.

Board and care homes serve as an important option for individuals who require assistance but prefer a more intimate setting than larger assisted living communities.

They can often provide a more affordable alternative to assisted living while still offering supervision and basic care services.

The smaller scale of these homes can create a family-like atmosphere that some residents find more comfortable and less overwhelming than larger facilities.

Assisted Living: Supportive Housing with Independence

Assisted living communities offer a middle ground. They provide housing, meals, supportive services, and some degree of healthcare, while promoting as much independence as possible.

Residents typically have their own apartments or rooms but benefit from 24-hour supervision and community activities.

These communities provide assistance with ADLs, medication management, transportation, and social activities.

Most offer three meals daily in communal dining rooms, housekeeping services, and security features.

Unlike nursing homes, assisted living communities generally do not provide complex medical care, though many now offer specialized memory care units for residents with dementia.

The assisted living model has evolved significantly in recent decades, with many communities now resembling upscale apartment communities rather than institutional settings. This evolution reflects growing consumer demand for environments that feel residential rather than medical, even as care needs increase.

Continuing Care Retirement Communities: A Comprehensive Approach

Continuing Care Retirement Communities (CCRCs) offer a unique approach by providing a continuum of housing and care options all on one campus.

Residents typically enter when still independent, often aged 55 or older, living in apartments or cottages, but can transition to assisted living or nursing care as needs change without having to relocate to a different community.

CCRCs generally require a substantial entrance fee plus monthly maintenance fees.

In exchange, they provide the security of knowing that increasing care needs can be accommodated within the same community.

This model appeals particularly to those who want to make a single move and then age in place as their needs evolve.

The financial structures of CCRCs vary significantly, with some offering guaranteed lifetime care for a fixed fee while others operate on a fee-for-service model where residents pay more as they require higher levels of care.

Understanding these contract differences is essential when considering a CCRC as part of a long-term plan.

Nursing Homes: Comprehensive Care for Complex Needs

Nursing homes provide the highest level of care outside a hospital setting, with 24-hour skilled nursing care for those with complex medical needs or severe cognitive impairments.

Modern nursing homes (also called skilled nursing facilities) offer both short-term rehabilitative care following hospitalizations and long-term custodial care for those with ongoing needs.

While nursing homes have historically been associated with institutional environments, many facilities are now evolving. This includes a shift toward more person-centered models that replace long, hospital-like wings with smaller, residential-style "households."

These settings emphasize private rooms, shared living areas, and consistent staffing to create a more familiar and dignified environment.

Despite these advancements, nursing home care remains the most restrictive and typically the most expensive care option. It is generally most appropriate for those with medical needs too complex to be managed in other settings or those requiring 24-hour supervision such as due to advanced dementia.

Interestingly, while a very small percentage of the total population resides in a nursing home, the likelihood increases significantly with age. Among Americans age 65 and older, only 1% of those aged 65-74 live in an institutional setting, rising to 2% for ages 75-84, and reaching 8% for those 85 and older.[12]

Memory Care: Specialized Support for Cognitive Impairment

Memory care units specialize in caring for those with Alzheimer's disease and other forms of dementia, with enhanced security features and specially trained staff. These units may exist within assisted living communities, nursing homes, or as standalone communities.

Memory care environments are designed specifically for the unique challenges of cognitive impairment.

They typically feature secure areas to prevent wandering, visual cues to aid navigation, specialized activity programming, and staff trained in dementia care techniques.

The physical environment is often designed to reduce confusion and agitation while promoting independence where possible.

As the number of Americans with Alzheimer's disease is projected to nearly double by 2050,[13] the demand for specialized housing has surged. Consequently, memory care has seen the highest rate of inventory growth in the senior living sector over the past decade, making it one of the most significant and rapidly expanding parts of the extended care continuum.[14]

THE STATISTICAL REALITY

Long-term care isn't a remote possibility. It's a statistical probability for most Americans. Data reveals that nearly 70% of adults who survive to age 65 will develop long-term care services and support needs at some point before they die, with approximately 42% receiving some form of paid care over their lifetime.[15]

> **KEY POINT:** Most long-term care begins at home, not in a facility. Creating a plan that supports care at home for as long as possible is what most people prefer and what long-term care planning should prioritize.

Simply being old does not imply a need for long-term care. However, as we age, the likelihood increases significantly, particularly after age 85.

When care is needed, the average duration differs significantly by gender: women typically need care for 3.7 years, while men average 2.2 years.[16]

Particularly noteworthy is the fact that 20% of today's 65-year-olds will need long-term care for more than five years.[17]

With average life expectancies continuing to increase and the last of the Baby Boomer generation reaching age 65 in 2030, the demand for extended care services is projected to surge dramatically in the coming decades.

The need for extended care isn't limited to the elderly. In fact, according to the CDC's National Study of Long-Term Care Providers, 37% of adult day services center participants are under age 65, a reminder that disability, chronic illness, and injury don't wait for retirement.[18]

This reality underscores that long-term care planning isn't just for seniors, it's relevant across the adult lifespan.

Several factors influence an individual's likelihood of needing long-term care:

- **Gender:** Women generally live longer than men and are more likely to live alone in their later years, increasing their probability of needing paid care services.

- **Longevity:** The longer you live, the more likely you are to develop conditions requiring assistance. Those with family histories of longevity should plan accordingly.

- **Health history:** Chronic conditions like diabetes, obesity, and hypertension increase the risk of disability later in life.

-  **Family situation:** The absence or limited availability of nearby family caregivers significantly increases the need for paid care services.

- **Genetic factors:** Family history of conditions like Alzheimer's disease may indicate increased risk.

Understanding these statistics isn't meant to alarm but to inform realistic planning. Extended care represents a significant risk that most families will face, one that can be managed with appropriate preparation.

BEYOND THE STATISTICS: REAL LIVES, REAL NEEDS

Statistics tell only part of the story. Behind each number is a person whose life has been fundamentally altered by the need for care, and a family often struggling to provide that care.

⊙ NAVIGATOR STORY

MARIA & ROBERT

Maria is a 72-year-old retired teacher who suffered a severe stroke. While she survived with her cognitive abilities intact, the stroke left her with significant mobility limitations.

She requires assistance with bathing, dressing, and meal preparation. Her husband Robert, himself 75, has become her primary caregiver—a role he was unprepared for and one that has taken a toll on his own health.

"I promised to love her in sickness and in health," Robert explains, "but I never imagined what that really meant. I'm exhausted all the time. Some days my arthritis is so bad I can barely help Maria into the shower. Our children want to help, but they live hours away and have their own families."

After six months of struggling alone, Robert finally arranged for a home care aide to visit three mornings a week. This professional help has made a significant difference, allowing Robert some respite and ensuring Maria receives consistent, quality care.

"I wish we had planned better for this possibility," Robert admits. "We saved diligently for retirement but never considered how we would manage if one of us needed care. The cost of even part-time help is substantial, and I worry about how long our savings will last if Maria's needs increase, let alone my future potential care needs."

 **NAVIGATOR STORY**

GABRIEL & FAMILY

Gabriel, a 63-year-old accountant, was diagnosed with early-onset Alzheimer's disease after colleagues noticed uncharacteristic errors in his work.

As his condition progressed, his wife Camila balanced her full-time job with increasing caregiving responsibilities, while their adult children, living in different states, struggled with how best to help from a distance.

"The hardest part was the unpredictability," Camila recalls. "Gabriel would have good days where he seemed almost normal, followed by days of confusion and agitation. I never knew what each day would bring, which made working and planning almost impossible."

After Gabriel wandered from home twice, the family reluctantly decided that a memory care facility would provide the specialized supervision he needed.

While the facility offers excellent care, the monthly cost exceeds $8,500—far more than the family had anticipated spending in their early 60s.

"We had disability insurance for income replacement when Gabriel could no longer work," Camila explains, "but nothing to cover the cost of his care. Our retirement plans have been completely upended, and I'm now facing difficult financial decisions I never expected to make at this stage of life."

These scenarios play out in millions of American households every day. Extended care isn't simply a matter of physical assistance. It involves complex emotional, financial, and logistical challenges that affect entire families.

THE CHANGING LANDSCAPE OF CARE

The long-term care landscape continues to evolve rapidly. Traditional models centered around institutional care are giving way to more flexible, person-centered approaches that leverage technology and community.

Today's Reality: A System Under Strain

The caregiver shortage, both professional and family, has reached crisis levels.[19] The "sandwich generation," adults simultaneously caring for aging parents and their own children, faces unprecedented stress and declining health themselves. The economic impact extends beyond families to employers and the broader economy through lost productivity, absenteeism, and workers forced to leave their jobs entirely to provide care. Meanwhile, the cost of care continues to rise faster than general inflation, putting quality care beyond the financial reach of many Americans.[20] [21]

Today's Technological Solutions

Current innovations in home care technology, telehealth, and community-based services are expanding options for those needing assistance. Remote monitoring systems now allow family members to check on loved ones from a distance. Medication management technologies help ensure proper dosing and timing. Smart home features can enhance safety and independence for those with physical limitations.

These technological advances are making it increasingly possible for people to remain in their homes even with significant care needs—a preference shared by the overwhelming majority of Americans.

Emerging Care Models

Alongside technology, new community-based models are taking root. The "village" concept brings together neighborhood residents to share services and support. Co-housing communities provide private homes with shared spaces and neighbor support built in. These models recognize that care isn't just about medical intervention. It's about maintaining social connection and purpose.

The Next Frontier: AI and Humanoid Caregivers

Within the next decade, artificial intelligence and humanoid robotics will fundamentally reshape how care is delivered and help solve the caregiver shortage crisis.

Humanoid caregivers, capable of assisting with physical tasks like lifting, turning, and mobility support, while also providing companionship and health monitoring, represent a highly probable and positive solution to the severe workforce gap. Countries like Japan and China are already integrating these technologies into national eldercare strategies.

As AI-powered robots become more sophisticated and affordable, the insurance industry will need to adapt its models, potentially reducing care costs through improved efficiency while redefining what constitutes covered care services. This isn't science fiction. It's an emerging reality that will make quality care more accessible and sustainable for millions of Americans who will need extended care in the coming decades.

What This Means for You

Understanding extended care means recognizing it as both a healthcare and a social issue—one that intersects with how we view aging, disability, family responsibility, and community support. The evolving landscape of care offers both promise and complexity.

As we move forward in this book, we'll explore not just the practical aspects of planning for extended care, but also the deeper questions about how we wish to live when we need assistance and how we can protect both our dignity and our financial security in this rapidly changing environment.

> **BOTTOM LINE:** Long-term care planning isn't just about preparing for a potential future need. It's about taking control of how that future will unfold, regardless of what health challenges may arise or what technological solutions become available.

☑ ACTION STEPS CHECKLIST

All worksheets and templates for this book are online at

WWW.YOURRETIREMENTBLINDSPOT.COM/RESOURCES

Complete them as digital forms or download PDFs. Scan the QR code here:

---

1. Complete the "Care Preferences Assessment" to identify your personal values regarding where and how you would want to receive care.

2. Use the "Local Resources Worksheet" to research and document home care agencies, adult day programs, assisted living communities, memory care, and skilled nursing options in your area.

3. Make a list of family members or friends who might be part of your care support network and their proximity to your home.

4. Start a conversation with your spouse or close family members about your care preferences and concerns.

5. Review the "Long-Term Care Glossary" in Appendix B to familiarize yourself with key terminology you'll encounter throughout this planning process.

THE REALITY OF
LONG-TERM CARE

- *Long-term care costs are substantial and rising faster than general inflation*

- *Retirement savings can be quickly depleted by long-term care expenses*

- *Family caregivers provide 80% of all care, often at large personal cost [22]*

- *Common misconceptions lead many to delay or avoid planning entirely*

- *The "care gap" means even those with financial resources may struggle to find quality care*

THE FINANCIAL BURDEN OF LONG-TERM CARE

The cost of long-term care represents one of the most significant financial risks facing Americans today.

Unlike many other expenses that can be predicted with reasonable accuracy, long-term care costs are characterized by uncertainty, both in terms of whether care will be needed and for how long.

Current national averages paint a sobering picture. As of 2025, the median annual costs for various care settings are:[23]

1.   Non-Medical In-Home Caregiver: $80,080 (based on 44 hours per week for 52 weeks)

2.   Adult Day Health Care: $24,700 (based on 5 days per week for 52 weeks)

3.   Assisted Living Community: $74,400 (room and board)

4.   Nursing Home: $114,975 (semi-private room) to $129,575 (private room)

These figures represent national medians, with significant regional variations. Urban areas on the East and West coasts typically see costs 20-40% higher than the national average, while some rural areas may have somewhat lower costs but often with more limited service availability.

Even more concerning is how rapidly these costs are climbing. From 2023 to 2024, assisted living costs surged 10%, nursing home costs rose 7-9%, and even home health aide services increased 3%, all significantly outpacing general inflation.[24]

At a 4% annual increase, today's $128,000 private nursing home room cost would grow to approximately $280,000 in just 20 years, far exceeding the median retirement savings of $200,000 for Americans aged 65-74.[25] [26]

A prolonged care need could easily deplete these savings, leaving surviving spouses financially vulnerable and eliminating any planned legacy for heirs.

In some cases, individuals find themselves needing to sell their homes to fund existing extended care scenarios, eliminating not only their financial cushion but also the primary asset they hoped to leave their beneficiaries.

THE HIDDEN COSTS: EMOTIONAL AND PHYSICAL IMPACT

The financial burden of extended care, while substantial, represents only part of the total cost.

The emotional and physical toll on family caregivers, often overlooked in financial planning, can be equally devastating.

Unpaid family caregivers provide approximately 80% of all long-term care in the United States, with an estimated economic value of $600 billion annually.[27]

Yet this statistic fails to capture the personal sacrifice involved:

- **Career Impact:** 70% of working-age family caregivers are employed while also providing care and experience work-related difficulties due to their caregiving responsibilities.[28] Many reduce their hours, pass up promotions, take leaves of absence, or exit the workforce entirely—decisions that carry significant long-term financial consequences.

- **Health Consequences:** The personal cost to family caregivers is substantial. They experience significantly higher rates of stress, depression, and anxiety than non-caregivers, with 25% reporting that caregiving has worsened their own health. [29] This chronic stress takes both a physical and psychological toll, with depression being especially common. Caring for someone with dementia creates even more severe health consequences than all other forms of caregiving.[30]

- **Relationship Strain:** The demands of caregiving frequently strain marriages and family relationships. Adult children caring for parents often find themselves navigating complex family dynamics, with siblings disagreeing about care decisions or unequal distribution of caregiving responsibilities.

> **KEY POINT:** Long-term care costs are rising faster than general inflation, typically 3-5% annually. This means the cost of care will likely be much higher when you actually need it than it is today.

 **NAVIGATOR STORY**

DMITRI

Dmitri became the primary caregiver for his wife following her Parkinson's diagnosis.

Over eight years, he watched as the vibrant, independent woman he married gradually lost her mobility and eventually her ability to communicate.

While deeply committed to her care, Dmitri experienced significant health problems of his own, including high blood pressure, insomnia, and depression.

Their retirement savings, intended to last another 25 years, were depleted in less than a decade.

"The hardest part wasn't the physical care or even watching my wife decline," Dmitri recalls. "It was the isolation. Friends stopped visiting. I couldn't leave the house for more than an hour. My world shrank to the size of our living room."

When Dmitri finally arranged for professional help, he was shocked by both the cost and the difficulty of finding qualified caregivers. "I waited too long to get help," he admits. "By then, I was physically and emotionally exhausted, and our financial options were limited. Had we planned ahead, we could have made very different choices."

 NAVIGATOR STORY

HANA

Hana moved her mother with advancing dementia into her home. While initially manageable, her mother's condition deteriorated to require round-the-clock supervision.

Hana reduced her work hours and eventually left her job entirely. The stress affected her marriage and her relationship with her teenage children, who felt neglected amid the constant demands of grandmother's care.

"I became a different person—always exhausted, quick to anger, constantly anxious," Hana explains. "My husband and I barely spoke except about mom's care. My kids started avoiding coming home. I felt like I was failing everyone, including my mother."

After eighteen months, Hana's family made the difficult decision to move her mother to a memory care facility. "The guilt was overwhelming at first," Hana says, "but it was the right decision for everyone. Mom actually receives better care now, and our family is healing. I just wish we'd had a plan in place before crisis hit."

These scenarios illustrate that extended care affects not just the care recipient but entire family systems—emotionally, physically, and financially.

BOTTOM LINE: The true cost of long-term care goes far beyond dollars. The emotional and physical toll on family caregivers, often called the "hidden victims" of a loved one's chronic illness, can be devastating and long-lasting.

CLEARING THE FOG: NAVIGATING THROUGH THE MISCONCEPTIONS

Successful navigation requires clear visibility and accurate charts.

Unfortunately, when it comes to long-term care planning, many Americans are making critical decisions based on misconceptions and outdated information rather than facts.

These misconceptions create a fog that obscures the reality of extended care needs and prevents effective planning.

> **BOTTOM LINE:** The most dangerous misconceptions about long-term care aren't just inaccurate — they actively prevent people from taking the steps necessary to protect themselves and their families.

Misconception 1: "It Won't Happen to Me"

Perhaps the most pervasive misconception is the belief that only *other* people need to worry about long-term care.

People tend to assume the risk is higher for someone else, not themselves, what psychologists call cognitive dissonance, the discomfort of holding two conflicting beliefs. We accept that most people will need care while simultaneously insisting it won't happen to us.

This self-protective thinking is especially common among men, who often see the need for care as incompatible with their identity as providers and protectors.

The reality: As we established in Chapter 1, extended care represents one of the most significant risks to retirement security and family stability for a majority of Americans.

Denial isn't just about ignoring the numbers. It's often rooted in deeper fears about losing independence, becoming a burden, or confronting mortality. Ironically, planning ahead actually preserves independence and relieves family members of the heaviest burdens.

 **NAVIGATOR STORY**

MALIK

Malik, a 74-year-old retired executive living in Southern California, prided himself on his physical fitness and independence. "I'll never need anyone to take care of me," he often told his wife and children. "I'll die with my boots on."

When a severe stroke left him partially paralyzed at 76, his family was emotionally and financially unprepared.

The stroke didn't kill him—it left him needing assistance with dressing, bathing, and mobility for the next four years.

"Dad's denial meant we had no plan," his daughter Sienna explains. "Mom aged ten years in two. She developed high blood pressure and chronic back pain from lifting him. My brother and I took turns flying in to give her breaks, but it caused tension about who was doing enough."

The financial impact was equally devastating. Malik's retirement income, already committed to living expenses and Medicare supplement premiums, now had to cover $6,500 monthly for a part-time home health aide.

To bridge the gap, they began systematically liquidating his investment portfolio, triggering capital gains taxes and permanently reducing their retirement income

By the time Malik passed, over $400,000 had been spent on care. His wife Yasmin was left with a depleted portfolio, ongoing health issues from caregiving, and the sobering reality that a portion of the legacy they'd planned to leave their children had been consumed by a risk Malik refused to acknowledge—and this was before considering her own potential long-term care needs.

Malik's story illustrates how denial doesn't change reality. It only prevents effective preparation for it.

Misconception 2: "Medicare Will Cover It"

A staggering 58% of Americans mistakenly believe Medicare will cover long-term care expenses, according to the 2025 Nationwide Retirement Institute survey.[31] This dangerous misconception leads many to assume they already have coverage when they actually face massive financial exposure.

> **KEY POINT:** Medicare was designed to address acute medical needs, not long-term custodial care. Expecting Medicare to cover long-term care is like expecting homeowner's insurance to pay for a housekeeper—it simply wasn't designed for that purpose.

The reality: Medicare provides very limited coverage for long-term care services. Specifically:

- Medicare pays for skilled nursing facility care for a maximum of 100 days, and only following a qualifying hospital stay of at least three days.

- Full coverage only applies for the first 20 days; for days 21-100, patients without supplemental coverage must pay a daily coinsurance of $217.00 (2026 rate).[32]

- Care must be "skilled" (rehabilitative) in nature, not custodial.

- Medicare provides limited home health care, but only when "medically necessary" and typically only a few hours per week.

- Medicare provides no coverage for assisted living communities.

- Medicare provides no coverage for long-term custodial care, which represents the vast majority of long-term care needs.

Misconception 3: "My Health Insurance Will Cover It"

Similar to the Medicare misconception, many working Americans mistakenly believe their private health insurance will cover extended care needs.

The reality: Traditional health insurance, like Medicare, focuses on medical treatment and rehabilitation, not custodial care. Private health insurance typically provides:

- Coverage for acute conditions and rehabilitative care

- Limited home health care for specific medical needs

- No coverage for assisted living communities

- No coverage for ongoing custodial care, whether at home or in a facility

Even the most comprehensive employer-based or private health insurance plans specifically exclude most extended care services, creating a significant coverage gap that many Americans don't discover until they actually need care.

Misconception 4: "My Family Will Take Care of Me"

Does your family know about this? Many Americans assume that family members, typically a spouse or adult children, will provide care if needed.

While this commitment comes from a place of love and devotion, it often overlooks the practical realities of modern caregiving.

The reality: Family caregiving comes with significant challenges:

- Geographic distance (many adult children live hours away from aging parents)

- Career demands (the majority of family caregivers are also employed)

- Lack of professional training (family caregivers typically have no formal preparation or credentials, leaving them ill-equipped for the demands of daily support)

- Smaller family sizes (fewer adult children to share responsibilities)

- Complex care needs that exceed a family member's capabilities

- The physical demands of caregiving, particularly for an elderly spouse

 Emotional and relationship strains that can permanently damage family dynamics

Moreover, family caregiving is rarely free. Family caregivers typically spend thousands of dollars annually on out-of-pocket expenses and often sacrifice income, benefits, and career advancement to provide care.

The hidden costs, both financial and personal, can be devastating to families who assumed care would simply be a matter of love and commitment.

⊙ NAVIGATOR STORY

SOPHIA

Sophia, a 48-year-old single mother, promised her father she would never put him in a care home. "Four years after my dad was diagnosed with an aggressive form of Multiple Sclerosis in his late sixties, his balance and strength had deteriorated to the point where he couldn't safely live alone anymore. I converted my dining room into a bedroom for him," she recalls.

"I had no idea what I was signing up for. Within a year, I had to reduce my work hours, my health was suffering, and my teenage son was resentful of the attention Dad required. We were all miserable, including my father, who hated feeling like a burden."

Eventually, Sophia found an assisted living community where her father could receive professional care. "It was the best decision for everyone. Dad thrives with professional care and social activities, and I can be his daughter again instead of his exhausted caregiver. I visit him several times a week, and our relationship is better than ever."

Misconception 5: "Long-Term Care Means a Nursing Home"

Many Americans equate long-term care exclusively with nursing homes, creating a major psychological barrier to planning. The thought, "I'll never go to a nursing home," often translates to "I don't need to plan for extended care."

The reality: As discussed in Chapter 1, long-term care encompasses a spectrum of services and settings. Currently:

- Less than 10% of people aged 85+ live in nursing homes[33]

- Most care is provided at home: 80% of elderly people receiving assistance live in private homes in the community, not in institutional settings[34]

- Assisted living and adult day care provide alternatives between home care and nursing homes

- Technological innovations continue to expand options for aging in place

Effective planning actually increases your control over where and how you receive care, making it more likely you can avoid a nursing home or delay the need for institutional care.

BOTTOM LINE: The question isn't whether you'll go to a nursing home—it's whether you want options about where and how you receive care if you need it.

Misconception 6: "I Can Self-Fund or Self-Insure If I Need Care"

Many middle-income and affluent individuals believe they can simply write a check if care is needed, often calling this "self-insuring."

But let's be clear: there's no actual insurance or leverage in this approach. Self-funding is just hoping for the best while facing potentially unlimited financial risks. You're simply assuming your assets will be enough, with no guarantees and no multiplier effect.

Here's the fundamental issue most people miss: long-term care isn't an asset problem. It's an income problem.

Think about it: What actually pays for care in real time? Not your portfolio balance. It's your cash flow. And if you're like most successful people, your income is already committed to covering your lifestyle obligations. Asking that same income to simultaneously pay for care and maintain all your other financial commitments is, in effect, double-counting it.

The reality: Self-funding and so-called "self-insuring" are fraught with hidden risks:

- **No leverage:** Unlike insurance, self-funding offers no way to multiply your dollars or transfer risk. You're on the hook for every expense, no matter how large.

- **Tax drag:** Liquidating investments to pay for care often triggers unnecessary taxes, shrinking your nest egg.

- **Market risk:** Needing care during a market downturn can force you to sell at a loss, permanently damaging your portfolio.

- **Legacy erosion:** Every dollar spent on care is one less for your spouse, heirs, or favorite causes.
- **No plan, just money:** Cash alone doesn't organize care, vet providers, or relieve your family from the burden of decision-making.

Most importantly, self-funding and "self-insuring" rarely address who will step in to coordinate care or make critical decisions. For families, these emotional and logistical burdens are often far more overwhelming than the financial ones.

We'll break down the pitfalls of self-funding—and why true insurance and leverage matter—in Chapter 4.

Misconception 7: "I'm Too Young to Worry About This"

Many Americans in their 40s, 50s, and 60s postpone extended care planning, believing it's an issue for much later in life.

The reality: Long-term care planning is most effective when addressed earlier:

- About 44% of home health care recipients are under age 65[35]
- Earlier planning provides more options and typically lower costs
- Health changes can happen suddenly and unexpectedly at any age
- Once health issues arise, many planning options become limited or unavailable

In reality, extended care planning is like retirement planning—the earlier you start, the more options you have and the less it typically costs.

Misconception 8: "Medicaid Will Cover My Care if Needed"

Some Americans assume Medicaid provides a reliable safety net for long-term care costs. In reality, Medicaid is a last-resort program with serious limitations, and even if you qualify, you may be forced to wait.

The reality: While Medicaid does cover long-term care services, it comes with significant drawbacks:

- Strict income and asset eligibility requirements that vary by state

- Limited choice of facilities, as many quality providers don't accept Medicaid

- Long waitlists for care in many areas; you may not get a bed when you need it

- Few home care options in most states

- Potential recovery from your estate after death

- Minimal protection for a healthy spouse's financial security

Medicaid was never designed as a planning strategy for middle-income or affluent families. It's a safety net for those with no other options, and even then, access is not guaranteed.

We'll examine Medicaid's role in long-term care financing more thoroughly in Chapter 5.

THE GROWING CARE GAP: A LOOMING CRISIS

As the population ages, the United States faces a widening gap between those needing care and those available to provide it. The surge in elderly Americans requiring long-term care services is colliding with a shrinking pool of caregivers to meet that demand.

Meanwhile, declining birth rates mean fewer family members available to provide unpaid care.

The professional caregiver workforce faces its own challenges: low wages, difficult working conditions, and limited career advancement opportunities have led to chronic shortages and high turnover rates.

This "care gap" means that even those with financial resources may struggle to find quality care when needed.

Planning must therefore consider not just how to pay for care but how to ensure access to preferred care settings and providers.

The care gap is particularly acute in rural areas, where the population is often older and services more limited. In some rural counties, there are no assisted living communities or home care agencies at all, forcing residents to relocate far from their communities when care is needed.

Even in urban areas with more providers, waiting lists for quality facilities are common. Those without advance planning often find themselves accepting whatever option is immediately available rather than what would best meet their needs and preferences.

THE RIPPLE EFFECT: HOW LONG-TERM CARE IMPACTS FAMILIES AND COMMUNITIES

Extended care needs rarely affect just one individual. When a person requires care, the repercussions extend to:

- **Spouses:** Often becoming unpaid caregivers while managing their own aging process and health concerns. Studies show that spousal caregivers over age 65 have a 63% higher mortality rate than non-caregivers of the same age.[36]

- **Adult Children:** Frequently caught between caregiving responsibilities and their own career and family obligations. This "sandwich generation," those simultaneously caring for aging parents and their own children, report particularly high levels of stress and financial strain.

- **Grandchildren:** May receive less financial support for education or see inheritance prospects diminished. The intergenerational impact of extended care costs can alter family financial trajectories for decades.

- **Employers:** Experience reduced productivity and increased absenteeism from employees with caregiving responsibilities. American businesses lose an estimated $33.6 billion annually in productivity due to employees' caregiving obligations.[37]

- **Communities:** Face increased demand for support services and, in some cases, charity care. As more individuals deplete their resources paying for care, the burden on community and government services grows.

The collective impact of unprepared individuals creates broader societal challenges, including strain on government programs, healthcare systems, and community resources. This makes long-term care planning not just a personal issue but a societal one as well.

BOTTOM LINE: Understanding the realities of long-term care isn't meant to frighten but to empower. Knowledge of the true landscape allows for thoughtful, proactive planning that can preserve both financial security and family well-being.

All worksheets and templates for this book are online at
WWW.YOURRETIREMENTBLINDSPOT.COM/RESOURCES
Complete them as digital forms or download PDFs. Scan the QR code here: 

———————

1. Calculate the cost of long-term care in your area using the Genworth Cost-of-Care Calculator at www.carescout.com/cost-of-care ☐

2. Identify which common misconceptions about long-term care you may have held. ☐

3. Make a list of the specific ways a long-term care event might impact your family members. ☐

4. Research caregiver support services in your community using the "Community Resources Worksheet." ☐

5. If you're currently providing care for someone, complete the "Caregiver Stress Assessment" to identify areas where you may need additional support. ☐

WHY PLAN NOW?

- *Health qualification for insurance becomes more difficult with age and declining health*

- *Planning early typically results in lower premiums and more comprehensive coverage*

- *Early planning expands choices about where and how you receive care*

- *Clear plans can reduce family conflict during already stressful times*

- *There are emotional benefits to having long-term care plans in place*

THE COST OF WAITING: HEALTH QUALIFICATION CHALLENGES

One of the most compelling reasons to plan for long-term care sooner rather than later is the simple reality of health qualification.

Unlike many financial products that become available to anyone willing to pay the price, both traditional long-term care insurance and hybrid long-term care products (which combine long-term care benefits with life insurance) require applicants to meet health qualification standards. The statistics are revealing...

Based on American Association for Long-Term Care Insurance (AALTCI) data, roughly 80% of applicants ages 50–59 are approved; approvals decline to about 70% at ages 60–64 and about 62% at ages 65–69. After age 70, nearly half are declined.[38]

Insurance companies assess **morbidity risk**—the likelihood you'll need care and for how long. For hybrid policies that include a life insurance component, they also evaluate **mortality risk**—how long you might live—since these products provide death benefits in addition to long-term care coverage.

Their underwriting processes have become increasingly sophisticated and stringent over time, making it more difficult to qualify as you age or develop health conditions.

Common conditions that can lead to application decline or premium increases include:

- **Mobility Issues:** Requiring a cane, walker, or wheelchair, or having a history of falls

- **Neurological Conditions:** Parkinson's disease, multiple sclerosis, seizure disorders, or early signs of cognitive decline (including mild cognitive impairment)

- **Cardiovascular History:** Recent heart attack, stroke, TIA (mini-stroke), congestive heart failure, or atrial fibrillation

- **Diabetes:** Especially with complications (neuropathy, retinopathy, kidney disease) or poor control

- **Osteoporosis:** Moderate to severe, particularly with a history of fractures

- **Cancer:** Recent diagnoses, ongoing treatments, or history of metastatic cancer

- **Obesity:** Particularly when combined with other health factors (hypertension, sleep apnea, diabetes)

- **Respiratory Disorders:** Chronic obstructive pulmonary disease (COPD), emphysema, or severe asthma

- **Kidney or Liver Disease:** Chronic kidney disease, dialysis, cirrhosis, or hepatitis

- **Mental Health Conditions:** Major depression, bipolar disorder, schizophrenia, or recent psychiatric hospitalizations

- **Medication Profile:** Taking multiple medications for chronic conditions, especially blood thinners, insulin, or narcotics

- **Substance Use:** History of alcohol or drug abuse

What makes this particularly challenging is that many of these conditions develop gradually and may not seem serious to the individual experiencing them.

A person might consider themselves "basically healthy" despite taking medication for high blood pressure, having mild arthritis, or experiencing occasional memory lapses.

Yet these seemingly minor issues can significantly impact insurability.

NAVIGATOR STORY

NAVIGATOR STORY: ELEANOR

Eleanor decided at age 62 that she should finally look into long-term care insurance.

Though she considered herself reasonably healthy despite taking medication for high blood pressure and mild arthritis, she was surprised to learn that her recent diagnosis of osteoporosis and a fall resulting in a broken wrist made her uninsurable with most carriers.

"I always thought I'd deal with long-term care planning someday," Eleanor explains. "I never realized 'someday' would arrive before I was ready—and before I could qualify for coverage at standard rates."

When Eleanor consulted with a certified long-term care specialist, she learned that had she applied a few years earlier, she likely would have qualified at standard rates. Now, her options were limited to a few carriers with higher premiums and more restrictive benefits.

"The specialist helped me find some coverage, but it was much more expensive than it would have been earlier, and I couldn't get all the features I wanted," Eleanor says. "My advice to friends now is simple: Don't wait. The best time to plan is when you're still healthy enough that you don't think you need to."

Though her long-term care policy represents a significant annual premium, she describes the peace of mind it provides as "priceless."

Eleanor's experience highlights a critical reality: Many people wait until they begin experiencing health issues to consider extended care planning, precisely when obtaining coverage becomes most difficult or expensive.

The ideal time to plan is when you're still healthy enough to qualify for the full range of options at the most favorable rates.

> **KEY POINT:** The best time to qualify for long-term care coverage is when you don't think you need it. Once health issues begin—even relatively minor ones—your options may become limited or more expensive.

FINANCIAL BENEFITS OF EARLY PLANNING

Beyond insurability concerns, there are significant financial advantages to addressing extended care planning early:

- **Lower Premiums:** All else being equal, the younger you are when you secure coverage, the lower your premiums will be. For traditional long-term care insurance, premiums can be substantially lower when purchased at age 50 versus age 65. For hybrid products, the internal rate of return on the long-term care benefit is more favorable with earlier purchase.

- **Compound Growth Potential:** Many long-term care policies offer inflation protection options that compound benefits over time. A 3% compound inflation option will double the benefit in approximately 24 years. The earlier you start, the more time this powerful growth has to work in your favor.

- **Budget Integration:** Incorporating long-term care premiums into your financial plan during peak earning years is often easier than trying to accommodate them in retirement when income may be fixed.

- **Protection of Other Financial Goals:** Early planning helps ensure that assets earmarked for other purposes—retirement income, education funding for grandchildren, charitable bequests—remain protected from potential care costs.

The Cost of Waiting

Financial professionals often refer to "the cost of waiting"—the tangible financial impact of delaying extended care planning. Each year of delay typically results in:

- Higher premiums for less coverage
- Fewer inflation protection options if health changes occur
- Reduced leverage on your investment
- Greater potential strain on retirement assets

For example, waiting just 10 years can mean paying 30-50% more in premiums while potentially qualifying for less comprehensive coverage due to health changes that commonly occur with age.

BOTTOM LINE: Starting your long-term care planning 10 years earlier can mean significantly more coverage at a lower cost. The power of compounding inflation protection alone makes earlier planning financially advantageous.

EXPANDED CHOICES: THE FREEDOM TO CHOOSE YOUR CARE

Perhaps the most valuable benefit of early planning is something money alone cannot buy: the freedom to choose how and where you receive care. Without adequate planning, care decisions are often made reactively during a crisis, limiting options and potentially leading to less desirable care settings.

When extended care needs arise suddenly, families often find themselves making critical decisions under extreme time pressure and emotional stress. The question becomes not "What would be best?" but rather "What's available right now?"

This reactive approach frequently results in care arrangements that no one, including the care recipient, would have chosen given more time and options.

Early planning expands choices in several critical ways:

- **Care Setting Options:** Comprehensive planning allows for consideration of the full spectrum of care settings—from home care to assisted living to specialized memory care—rather than being limited to whatever has immediate availability during a crisis.

- **Provider Selection:** With proper planning, families can research and select care providers based on quality, reputation, and fit with personal preferences rather than simply accepting whoever has capacity.

- **Location Flexibility:** Planning ahead allows consideration of care options near family members or in preferred communities, rather than being limited to the immediate geographic area during a crisis.

- **Continuity of Care:** A well-designed plan can provide for smooth transitions between levels of care as needs change, rather than disruptive moves dictated by financial or availability constraints.

◉ NAVIGATOR STORY

LIAM & LEILA

Liam and Leila, a couple in their mid-50s, created their long-term care plan after watching Liam's mother struggle to find appropriate care for his father.

"Mom had to place Dad in the only nursing home with an immediate opening, 45 minutes from their home," Liam recalls. "It was a terrible fit—understaffed, institutional, and so far away that Mom could only visit twice a week. Dad was miserable, and Mom was consumed with guilt."

Determined to avoid a similar situation, Liam and Leila worked with a certified long-term care specialist to create a comprehensive plan that included both insurance coverage and detailed care preferences. When Leila was unfortunately diagnosed with Alzheimer's disease at age 76, their advance planning made all the difference.

"Because we had planned ahead, we had both the financial resources and the time to find the right care situation," Liam explains. "Leila was able to remain home with family caregiving and some custodial care for three years. When that was no longer feasible as her condition progressed, we found an assisted living community with a specialized memory care program just ten minutes from our daughter's home. The contrast with my father's experience couldn't be more stark."

Their story illustrates how early planning creates options that simply aren't available in crisis situations. The freedom to choose care that aligns with personal preferences and values is perhaps the most significant benefit of proactive planning.

FAMILY HARMONY: PREVENTING CONFLICT AND RESENTMENT

Another compelling reason to plan now is the impact on family relationships. Clear plans for potential care needs significantly reduce the likelihood of family conflict during already stressful times.

When no plan exists, adult children often find themselves making difficult decisions about a parent's care with little guidance about what the parent would have wanted. This frequently leads to disagreements about:

- **Appropriate Level of Care:** Siblings may disagree about whether a parent needs facility care or can remain at home with support.

- **Financial Responsibility:** Without clear funding plans, conflicts often arise about who should pay for care and how assets should be used.

- **Caregiving Responsibilities:** Care duties frequently fall unevenly on adult children, with those living closest or with fewer competing responsibilities shouldering the greatest burden.

- **Medical Decisions:** Without advance directives and clear communication, family members may have different interpretations of a parent's wishes regarding medical interventions.

These conflicts can create lasting damage to sibling relationships and other family bonds. In extreme cases, families become permanently estranged over disagreements about care decisions and financial responsibilities. It's often been said, long-term care doesn't bring families together, it can tear them apart.

Early planning prevents many of these conflicts by:

- **Clarifying Preferences:** Documenting specific wishes about care settings, treatment approaches, and quality-of-life priorities.

- **Establishing Financial Resources:** Creating dedicated funding for care needs, removing financial pressure from family members.

- **Designating Decision-Makers:** Clearly identifying who has authority to make decisions if the individual cannot.

- **Setting Expectations:** Helping family members understand roles and responsibilities before a crisis occurs.

⊕ NAVIGATOR STORY

THE COHEN SIBLINGS

The Cohen siblings—Ethan, Rachel, and Noah—experienced firsthand how the absence of planning can fracture family relationships. When their mother developed dementia, no plan existed for her care or finances.

"Mom always avoided discussions about aging or illness," Rachel explains. "She never created advance directives or discussed her preferences with any of us. When she could no longer make decisions for herself, we had no roadmap to follow."

The result was years of conflict. Ethan, who lived closest, believed their mother should move to a memory care community. Rachel, who had medical training, advocated for home care with professional support. Noah, who lived across the country, primarily focused on preserving their mother's assets.

"We argued constantly," Ethan recalls. "Every decision became a battle. Rachel and I barely speak now, and Noah hasn't visited in years. Mom would be heartbroken to see what happened to our family."

Their experience contrasts sharply with families who benefit from advance planning. When care preferences, financial resources, and decision-making authority are clearly established, families can focus on supporting their loved one and each other rather than arguing about fundamental decisions.

PEACE OF MIND: THE EMOTIONAL VALUE OF PLANNING

While the practical benefits of early planning are substantial, the emotional benefits may be equally significant. There is profound peace of mind that comes from knowing you've taken steps to protect yourself and your loved ones from one of life's most significant financial and emotional risks.

This peace of mind manifests in several ways:

- **Reduced Anxiety:** Knowing that a plan exists for potential care needs significantly reduces worry about the future, allowing for greater enjoyment of the present.

- **Empowerment:** Taking control of future care decisions creates a sense of agency and self-determination, countering the helplessness often associated with aging and potential dependency.

- **Family Reassurance:** Adult children gain tremendous peace of mind knowing their parents have planned for potential care needs, reducing worry about both their parents' wellbeing and their own potential caregiving responsibilities.

- **Legacy Protection:** Planning helps ensure that the legacy you wish to leave, both financial and emotional, remains intact regardless of care needs.

◉ NAVIGATOR STORY

JEREMY & JULIE

Jeremy and Julie, a couple in their mid-50s, decided to address long-term care planning after watching Jeremy's parents struggle with his father's recovery from a major stroke. The experience of seeing his mother's health decline under the stress of caregiving and their retirement savings rapidly deplete motivated them to create their own plan."

After what we witnessed with my parents, we couldn't ignore this issue," Jeremy explains. "My mother essentially sacrificed her own health caring for my father. We don't want to put ourselves or our children in the same impossible predicament."

Because they planned in their mid-50s while still in good health, they were able to secure comprehensive coverage with premiums that fit comfortably into their financial plan. They describe the peace of mind it provides as "priceless."

THE POWER OF INFORMATION AND OPTIONS

Another compelling reason to begin planning now is the advantage of time—time to research, understand options, and make thoughtful decisions rather than rushed ones.

Long-term care planning involves complex choices, such as:

- **Coverage Approach:** Traditional long-term care insurance versus hybrid products

- **Benefit Structure:** Daily or monthly benefit amounts, benefit periods, elimination periods

- **Inflation Protection:** Simple versus compound, various percentage options

- **Care Coordination:** Services to help navigate the care system when needed

- **Joint Coverage:** Individual policies versus shared benefit approaches for couples

Each of these decisions benefits from careful consideration, consultation with knowledgeable professionals, and discussions with family members. Starting the planning process early allows for this deliberate approach.

Additionally, the long-term care marketplace continues to evolve, with new products and features regularly introduced.

Those who begin the education process early are better positioned to evaluate innovations and determine which solutions best align with their personal circumstances and preferences.

Early planning also provides time to explore and understand the care resources available in your community.

This knowledge becomes invaluable when care needs arise, as you'll already be familiar with local providers, their specialties, and their quality reputations.

PLANNING AS AN ACT OF LOVE

Perhaps the most powerful reason to plan now is one that transcends financial calculations: **planning for long-term care is fundamentally an act of love toward both yourself and your family.**

For yourself, it represents a commitment to dignity, choice, and quality of life even during vulnerable times.

> **KEY POINT:** Long-term care planning isn't a single decision but a process that benefits from time, information, and careful consideration. Starting early allows you to make thoughtful choices rather than rushed decisions during a crisis.

It acknowledges that your preferences and values matter, regardless of your physical or cognitive condition.

For your family, it demonstrates foresight and consideration, sparing them difficult decisions, financial burdens, and the strain of unplanned caregiving.

A comprehensive plan allows your loved ones to serve as care coordinators rather than hands-on caregivers—enabling them to oversee your care with clarity and purpose instead of becoming physically and emotionally depleted by providing daily personal care.

It allows them to focus on providing emotional support rather than struggling with logistical and financial challenges.

When viewed through this lens, extended care planning becomes less about preparing for decline and more about ensuring that your final chapters are written on your terms, with the resources necessary to support your vision of aging with dignity and grace.

This perspective aligns with what gerontologists call "successful aging"—approaching later life with intention, adaptability, and resilience.[39]

Long-term care planning becomes not just a financial strategy but an integral part of how we choose to age well.

> **BOTTOM LINE:** Long-term care planning is ultimately an act of love—for yourself and for those who care about you. It preserves dignity, choices, and relationships during what could otherwise be a time of crisis and conflict.

TAKING THE FIRST STEP

The journey of long-term care planning begins with a single step: recognizing the significant risk associated with the potential need for extended care and committing to proactively address it.

> **KEY POINT:** The best long-term care plan is one created long before it's needed. By taking action today, you're investing in security, dignity, and peace of mind for tomorrow.

By engaging with this material and taking the time to read this book, you're already demonstrating a commendable commitment to understanding the complexities of long-term care.

This doesn't mean you need to purchase a policy immediately or make all decisions at once.

Rather, it means beginning the education process, assessing your personal risk factors, and exploring the options available to you.

In the following sections of this book, we'll guide you through this process step by step, from understanding funding options to creating a personalized plan that aligns with your values, preferences, and financial circumstances.

The key is to begin now, while time is on your side, your health remains an asset, and the full range of planning options remains available to you.

☑ ACTION STEPS CHECKLIST

All worksheets and templates for this book are online at
WWW.YOURRETIREMENTBLINDSPOT.COM/RESOURCES
Complete them as digital forms or download PDFs. Scan the QR code here:

———————

1. Schedule a health assessment to understand your current insurability status. ☐

2. Complete the "Long-Term Care Risk Assessment" to identify your personal risk factors. ☐

3. Calculate how much you could save by planning now versus waiting 5-10 years using the "Cost of Waiting Calculator." ☐

4. Make a list of the specific choices and control you want to maintain if you ever need care. ☐

5. Set a deadline for exploring long-term care coverage options with a qualified specialist. ☐

PAYING FOR LONG-TERM CARE

Understanding the various funding options for long-term care—from self-funding to government programs to insurance solutions—allows you to make informed decisions that align with your financial resources, values, and care preferences.

Each approach carries distinct advantages, limitations, and trade-offs that must be carefully evaluated within the context of your overall financial plan.

By examining these options systematically, you can develop a strategy that protects both your assets and your family's well-being while preserving your autonomy and dignity.

THE RISKS OF RELYING ON SELF-FUNDING

- *The "myth of self-funding" often overlooks critical financial risks*

- *Liquidating assets to pay for care can trigger a cascade of unintended tax consequences—income taxes, capital gains, increased Social Security taxation, and Medicare premium surcharges—that compound the true cost of self-funding*

- *Long-term care costs can deplete even substantial portfolios, especially during market downturns*

- *Withdrawing large sums during market corrections creates devastating "sequence of returns" risk*

- *Surviving spouses face financial vulnerability if care depletes joint assets*

- *Leveraged insurance solutions provide significantly multiplied care benefits compared to dollar-for-dollar self-funding*

- *Self-assuring offers a path between self-funding and traditional insurance*

THE MYTH OF SELF-FUNDING

A statement frequently heard from affluent individuals, reflects one of the most common and potentially costly misconceptions in retirement planning: *"I have enough money to self-fund my long-term care needs."*

While having substantial assets certainly provides greater financial flexibility, true self-funding of long-term care involves risks that many fail to fully appreciate.

Self-funding means setting aside assets to pay for potential care needs out-of-pocket if and when they arise.

At first glance, this approach seems straightforward—why pay insurance premiums for something you might never need when you could simply use your own money if necessary?

However, this perspective often overlooks several critical factors that can undermine even well-funded retirement plans.

The decision to self-fund extended care expenses isn't simply about having a large enough portfolio; it's about understanding the complex interplay between care costs, market volatility, longevity risk, and the impact on surviving family members. Put simply, self-funding is hoping for the best while taking on unlimited financial risk. Even before considering market conditions, there's a cost most people overlook: taxes.

BOTTOM LINE: Self-funding isn't simply a matter of having "enough" money. It's about whether your assets will be accessible and sufficient when needed, potentially under adverse market conditions, and what the impact will be on your surviving spouse and other financial goals.

THE HIDDEN TAX TOLL OF SELF-FUNDING

The decision to self-fund typically focuses on a single question: *Do I have enough?* But that question ignores a critical reality—it's not just about having the money, it's about what it costs to access it.

When you liquidate assets to pay for care, you don't just spend money. You trigger a cascade of tax consequences that can dramatically increase the true cost of self-funding.

The Tax Hit on Withdrawals

Retirement accounts—IRAs, 401(k)s, 403(b)s—were designed to provide income over decades, not to be drained in a care crisis. Every dollar withdrawn is taxed as ordinary income. Large withdrawals can push you into a higher tax bracket, meaning you're not just paying taxes, you're paying *more* taxes per dollar than you would under normal retirement distributions..

Capital Gains on Liquidated Investments

Selling appreciated assets in a taxable brokerage account triggers capital gains taxes. You don't control *when* you need care, which means you don't control *when* you're forced to sell. You may be liquidating at the worst possible time: during a market downturn, locking in losses, or during a peak, triggering a large taxable gain.

The Social Security Tax Trap

Higher income from retirement account withdrawals or capital gains increases your "combined income"—the figure used to determine how much of your Social Security benefits are taxable. Up to 85% of your Social Security can become taxable income, creating a domino effect: you pull money for care, which increases your income, which makes more of your Social Security taxable, which increases your income further.

Medicare Premium Surcharges (IRMAA)

For those 65 and older, there's another layer. Medicare Part B and Part D premiums aren't flat. They're income-adjusted. Liquidating assets to pay for care increases your Modified Adjusted Gross Income (MAGI), which can trigger Income-Related Monthly Adjustment Amounts (IRMAA). These surcharges can add hundreds of dollars per month to your Medicare premiums, and they're based on income from two years prior, meaning a single high-income year can impact your premiums for years afterward.

The Charitable Deduction You'll Never Take

For those who tithe or make regular charitable contributions, self-funding creates a silent cost: every dollar used to pay for care is a dollar that can't go to charity, and a dollar that can't generate a charitable deduction. The tax benefit of giving is quietly eliminated.

BOTTOM LINE: The true cost of self-funding includes income taxes, capital gains, Social Security taxation, Medicare surcharges, and lost deductions. Tax-free LTC insurance benefits avoid all of them.

PORTFOLIO DEPLETION ANALYSIS: THE MATHEMATICS OF UNCERTAINTY

Long-term care represents a unique financial risk because of three key characteristics: its high cost, its uncertain duration, and its potential to occur during market downturns. These factors interact to create significant risk even for substantial portfolios.

KEY POINT: The timing of long-term care needs relative to market performance can be more important than the total amount of assets you've accumulated. Withdrawing large sums during market downturns can severely test the resilience of even substantial portfolios.

Consider a hypothetical couple, Marco and Max, both age 65, with $2 million in retirement assets. They estimate they'll need $80,000 per year, a 4% withdrawal rate, to maintain their lifestyle. Confident in their planning, they assume their assets are more than sufficient to handle any care needs that might arise.

Even with prudent investment management, their $2 million portfolio isn't guaranteed to last through a 30-year retirement—and that's before accounting for any extended care costs.

But what happens if Max requires three years of assisted living and home care beginning at age 82? Based on current national averages, assisted living plus part-time home health aide support can easily exceed $100,000 annually, and when adjusted for healthcare inflation, these costs could more than double by the time Max needs care.

If this occurs during a period of market stability, the additional withdrawals reduce their portfolio's sustainability, but they still maintain a reasonable probability of their assets lasting through age 95.

The picture changes dramatically if Max needs the same care during a significant market downturn—after their portfolio has already declined by 25%.

The combination of reduced assets and increased withdrawals during a down market creates what financial professionals call "sequence of returns" risk. This means the timing of withdrawals matters as much as the amount. Their probability of maintaining income through age 95 drops substantially—potentially by half or more—and Marco faces a significant risk of outliving their assets.

This simplified analysis demonstrates that even substantial portfolios can be vulnerable to the combined impact of extended care costs and market volatility. The real risk isn't simply whether you have "enough" money in theory, but whether those assets will be accessible and sufficient when needed—especially under adverse market conditions.

IMPACT ON SURVIVING SPOUSES: THE HIDDEN VULNERABILITY

As briefly discussed in the previous example, when long-term care needs arise for one spouse, the financial implications for the surviving spouse are often overlooked in planning discussions. This oversight represents one of the most significant potential consequences of inadequate long-term care planning.

Consider a hypothetical scenario: A husband requires extended care for several years, depleting a significant portion of the couple's assets. After his death, his widow must continue her retirement with substantially reduced resources.

Women, who typically live longer than men and are more likely to spend their final years alone, are particularly vulnerable to this risk.

The financial impact extends beyond simple dollar amounts. The surviving spouse may face:

- Reduced income for basic living expenses
- Inability to remain in the family home
- Dependence on adult children for financial support
- Limited options if they subsequently need care themselves
- Inability to leave intended legacies to children or charities

 NAVIGATOR STORY

MIRIAM

Miriam's story illustrates this reality. When her husband was diagnosed with congestive heart failure and early signs of dementia at age 72, they initially managed his care at home. As his condition progressed, he required frequent medical supervision and daily assistance with basic activities.

Over time, they hired home health aides and eventually moved him to an assisted living community with a dedicated memory care unit that could provide comprehensive support for both his mobility challenges and increasing cognitive needs. Over seven years, they spent approximately $600,000 on his care—nearly half their retirement savings.

"We had planned so carefully for our retirement," Miriam recalls. "But our financial advisor never asked us, 'what if one of you needs care for years?' It simply wasn't part of the conversation."

After his death, Miriam, then 80, found herself with a dramatically reduced portfolio generating significantly less income than their original retirement plan had projected. She was forced to sell their home and move to a smaller apartment. When she later developed her own care needs, her options were severely limited by her reduced financial resources.

"I always thought I'd be financially comfortable for my whole life," she says. "Instead, I worry constantly about running out of money or becoming a burden to my children."

THE TRUE COST OF SELF-FUNDING VS. LEVERAGED SOLUTIONS

Self-funding long-term care means paying dollar-for-dollar for all care costs.

In contrast, insurance-based solutions provide leverage—the ability to receive more in benefits than you pay in premiums if care is needed.

Self-Funding Approach

- You might set aside $100,000 (after-tax, non-IRA) in a conservative investment for potential care needs.

- If care is needed, you spend the $100,000 plus any growth.

- If care is never needed, the $100,000 plus any growth remains in your estate.

- If care costs exceed $100,000, you must tap your income-producing portfolio—potentially during a market downturn—with no ceiling on your exposure. There is no stop loss.

Leveraged Insurance Approaches

Traditional Long-Term Care Insurance

- You pay annual premiums, which vary based on your age, health, and coverage design.

- If care is needed, you access substantially more in benefits than your total premium payments, often providing the highest leverage ratio of all options since the entire premium goes toward care benefits. This option is pure insurance.

- If care is never needed, premiums paid are generally not recoverable.

- This approach maximizes the long-term care benefit amount per premium dollar and can provide comprehensive coverage with inflation protection.

Hybrid Long-Term Care Policy

You reposition assets (like $100,000) into a hybrid long-term care policy.

- If care is needed, you may access substantially more in long-term care benefits than your initial premium. Many policies offer multiple times your premium in potential benefits, with the exact amount depending on your age, health, and policy design.

- This actually creates the stop loss that self-funding lacks. The first $100,000 in benefits comes from your own repositioned dollars. But once that's exhausted, the insurance company pays the remainder, providing a multiple of your premium in additional benefits. Your exposure is capped; your protection is multiplied, creating the stop loss.

- If care is never needed, your beneficiaries receive a tax-free death benefit (often equal to your original premium), or the cash value remains in your estate.

■ This approach addresses the "use it or lose it" concern while still providing significant leverage against care costs.

While no policy can guarantee full protection against all possible care costs or durations, both insurance approaches provide a significant financial buffer. They help offset the risk of extended or catastrophic care scenarios, with many policies offering benefits for multiple years or even lifetime coverage.

BOTTOM LINE: Self-funding means you pay dollar-for-dollar for care costs, while insurance solutions can provide multiple times more benefit for the same investment.

SELF-ASSURING: ANOTHER WAY TO THINK ABOUT THE STOP LOSS

Another way to frame the stop-loss concept is through a strategy that helps clarify what you're actually accomplishing with this approach.

"Self-assuring"—a strategy credited to Shawn Britt, CLU, CLTC, at Nationwide[40], describes a funding approach using hybrid long-term care policies that emphasizes this stop-loss positioning.

Self-funding means taking on unlimited risk with no leverage. Traditional long-term care insurance provides maximum leverage but requires ongoing premiums, and if care is never needed, those premiums are gone.

Self-assuring, by contrast, uses hybrid products to create a different outcome.

How self-assuring works:

- Repositions existing assets rather than committing to ongoing premiums
- Creates leverage—access to multiples of your premium if care is needed
- Returns funds to heirs via death benefit or cash value if care is never needed
- Eliminates "use it or lose it" risk
- Maintains liquidity and control over your assets
- Transfers the financial risk of extended care to an insurance company

Self-assuring repositions your assets to create leverage and a stop loss, potentially protecting against a significant portion of long-term care costs while preserving value for your heirs if care is never needed.

THE PSYCHOLOGICAL IMPACT: FROM CONFIDENCE TO CONCERN

Beyond the financial implications, self-funding creates psychological burdens that many fail to anticipate.

As retirement progresses and the possibility of needing care becomes more immediate, what once seemed like "plenty of money" may begin to feel less secure.

This shifting perspective often leads to:

- Increased anxiety about potential care costs

- More conservative spending in other areas of life
- Reluctance to enjoy retirement fully for fear of depleting resources
- Stress about becoming a burden on family members
- Concern about legacy goals being compromised

In contrast, those with leveraged protection often report greater peace of mind and willingness to enjoy their retirement assets, knowing that a significant portion of their care risk has been transferred to an insurance company.

WHEN SELF-FUNDING MAKES SENSE

Despite the risks outlined above, self-funding may be appropriate in certain circumstances:

- Ultra-high-net-worth individuals with assets well beyond their lifetime needs
- Those with significant guaranteed income sources (pensions, annuities) that could cover potential care costs
- Individuals with health conditions that make them uninsurable
- Those with strong family support systems and clear agreements about care provision

It is imperative, however, that even those who choose to self-fund establish a comprehensive, documented long-term care plan—one that clearly delineates funding mechanisms, care locations, and coordination responsibilities.

Without such strategic planning, even the most substantial

financial resources may prove insufficient in securing quality care when it matters most.

THE RATIONAL APPROACH: RISK MANAGEMENT, NOT PREDICTION

The decision to self-fund long-term care often stems from an optimistic belief: "I probably won't need care," or "If I do, it won't be for long."

While this optimism is understandable, it represents a prediction-based approach rather than a risk management approach.

Effective financial planning doesn't attempt to predict specific outcomes but rather manages the consequences of various possibilities.

We don't insure our homes because we expect them to burn down, but because we can't afford the consequences if they do.

Similarly, long-term care planning isn't about predicting whether you'll need care. It's about ensuring that if you do, you'll have access to the quality care you deserve without compromising your financial security, your dignity, or burdening your loved ones.

> **KEY POINT:** Extended care planning is risk management, not prediction. It's not about whether you'll need care—it's about being prepared if you do. The question isn't "Will I need care?" but rather "If I need care, do I have a plan that protects my family and finances?"

☑ ACTION STEPS CHECKLIST

All worksheets and templates for this book are online at
WWW.YOURRETIREMENTBLINDSPOT.COM/RESOURCES
Complete them as digital forms or download PDFs. Scan the QR code here:

———————

1. Complete a portfolio stress test to evaluate how various care scenarios would impact your retirement savings.

2. Calculate the annual income your portfolio generates and determine how much would be redirected if care costs arose.

3. Identify which financial goals or commitments would be most at risk if you needed to self-fund long-term care.

4. Discuss with your spouse or partner the potential impact on the surviving spouse if care depletes joint assets.

5. Compare the leverage advantage of insurance solutions against self-funding for your specific situation.

GOVERNMENT PROGRAMS – WHAT THEY OFFER AND WHAT THEY DON'T

CHAPTER AT A GLANCE

- *Medicare covers only limited, short-term skilled nursing care, not long-term custodial care*

- *Medicaid covers long-term care only after nearly all assets are depleted*

- *Long-Term Care Partnership Programs offer asset protection for those who purchase qualifying private insurance*

- *Veterans' benefits provide limited financial assistance for qualifying wartime veterans*

- *PACE (Program of All-Inclusive Care for the Elderly) offers comprehensive community-based care but has limited availability and eligibility requirements*

- *Government programs should be a safety net, not a key funding strategy*

THE MEDICARE MISCONCEPTION

Perhaps the most pervasive and costly misconception in long-term care planning is the belief that Medicare will cover long-term care needs.

Recent research from the Nationwide Retirement Institute reveals that nearly 60% of adults with household incomes over $75,000 incorrectly assume Medicare will cover their long-term care expenses.

This misunderstanding creates significant financial exposure for families who haven't made alternative arrangements.[41]

Medicare's Purpose and Limitations

Medicare, the federal health insurance program primarily for people age 65 and older, is designed to address acute medical needs—such as hospital stays, physician visits, and short-term rehabilitation—not long-term custodial care.[42]

Understanding these limitations is essential for realistic extended care planning.

What Medicare Does and Doesn't Cover

Skilled Nursing Facility (SNF) Care: Medicare Part A will pay for skilled nursing facility care, but only under very specific circumstances:

- The care must follow a qualifying hospital stay of at least three consecutive days as an inpatient (not under observation status).

- Admission to the skilled nursing facility must occur within 30 days of hospital discharge.

- The care needed must be skilled nursing or rehabilitation services, and the patient must show improvement potential.

When these conditions are met, Medicare covers:

- Days 1–20: Medicare pays 100% of covered services.

- Days 21–100: Medicare pays all but a daily coinsurance amount ($217.00 per day in 2026).

- Beyond 100 days: Medicare pays nothing.[43]

What Medicare Does NOT Cover

- Long-term custodial care: Medicare does not cover help with activities of daily living (ADLs) such as bathing, dressing, or eating when this is the primary need.[44]

- Supervision for dementia: Medicare does not pay for care when the primary need is supervision rather than skilled medical treatment, which is particularly relevant for those with dementia.

- Assisted living facility costs: Medicare provides no coverage for assisted living or most home care services unless they are part of a prescribed, medically necessary treatment plan.

> **KEY POINT:** Medicare covers short-term, rehabilitative skilled care, not long-term custodial care. Its coverage is limited to 100 days maximum, with substantial co-payments required after the first 20 days.

The Gap Between Medicare Coverage and Actual Care Needs

Medicare's coverage limitations become particularly problematic when compared to the actual duration of care many seniors require.

For perspective, government research from the Department of Human Services and National Center for Health Statistics reveals a sobering reality: the typical nursing home stay extends to approximately 485 days, over 16 months of care. More critically, the majority of residents (57%) require care beyond Medicare's 100-day coverage limit, leaving families financially exposed for months or even years of expensive care costs without adequate planning.[45]

Additionally, many long-term care needs do not begin with a qualifying hospital stay, making Medicare coverage unavailable from the outset.

Medicare Advantage and Medigap

Some Medicare Advantage plans have begun offering limited long-term care benefits, such as home care assistance or adult day care services. However, these benefits are typically capped at low dollar amounts or limited service hours and are not designed to address catastrophic or lengthy care needs.[46]

Medicare Supplement (Medigap) policies help cover Medicare deductibles and copayments but follow Medicare's same coverage rules and limitations. They do not expand long-term care coverage.[47]

 **NAVIGATOR STORY**

DARIUS & MALIA

Darius and Malia had always assumed Medicare would cover most of their healthcare needs in retirement, including any long-term care. When Darius suffered a debilitating stroke at age 78, he initially received excellent acute care through Medicare. After his hospitalization, he was transferred to a skilled nursing facility for rehabilitation.

"The first 20 days went smoothly," Malia recalls. "Then we started getting bills for over $200 per day. When we asked questions, we discovered Medicare's coverage was limited. We had no idea."

After 73 days, Darius's Medicare coverage ended completely when his therapists determined he had reached a "plateau" in his recovery. Though he still needed considerable assistance with daily activities, Medicare would no longer cover his care because it was now considered custodial, not rehabilitative.

"We had to move Darius back home before we were ready because we couldn't afford $9,000 a month out-of-pocket," says Malia. "I became his primary caregiver overnight, with no training and little support. Medicare paid for nothing after that."

> **BOTTOM LINE:** Medicare's coverage for long-term care is far more limited than most people realize. It covers only short-term, skilled care following a hospital stay—not the long-term custodial care that most people eventually need.

MEDICAID: THE SAFETY NET WITH STRINGS ATTACHED

Medicaid is the nation's largest payer of long-term care, but it's not a universal solution—it's a safety net for those with limited means.

To qualify, you must meet strict financial and medical criteria. In most states, this means having less than $2,000 in countable assets if you're single. If you're married and only one spouse needs care, the "community spouse" can keep more, typically between $30,000 and $150,000, depending on the state.[48]

Qualifying for Medicaid isn't just about your current finances. The program reviews your financial transactions over the past five years. Gifts or transfers for less than fair market value can trigger a penalty period, delaying your eligibility.[49]

Once eligible, Medicaid will cover nursing home care in approved facilities, and in many states, home and community-based services (HCBS) are available through special waiver programs. However, coverage for assisted living is limited and varies widely by state.[50]

Wait Lists: A Hidden Barrier

Even after qualifying for Medicaid, access to care isn't always immediate. Many states have long wait lists for home and community-based services (HCBS) such as in-home care, adult day care, or assisted living. As of 2024, over 700,000 people nationwide were on wait lists for Medicaid HCBS waivers, with average waits ranging from months to several years depending on the state and service.[51]

> **KEY POINT:** Medicaid is means-tested, requiring you to spend down nearly all your assets before qualifying. While it provides essential care for those without resources, it significantly limits your choices about where and how you receive care.

For nursing home care, wait lists can also occur, especially in areas where few facilities accept Medicaid or where Medicaid beds are limited. Not all facilities accept Medicaid patients, and those that do often maintain limited Medicaid beds.

This reality can force difficult choices: waiting for an available spot, being placed in a facility far from family and support networks, or facing quality concerns at facilities that rely heavily on Medicaid funding, as reimbursement rates are typically lower than private pay rates.

Another important consideration is estate recovery. After a Medicaid recipient passes away, states are required to seek repayment for long-term care costs from the person's estate, often by placing a lien on the home or other assets. This can significantly reduce what's left for heirs.[52]

> **BOTTOM LINE:** Medicaid is an essential safety net for those who exhaust their resources, but it comes with significant trade-offs in choice, access, and legacy.

LONG-TERM CARE PARTNERSHIP PROGRAMS: A PUBLIC-PRIVATE SOLUTION

Partnership Programs represent a collaboration between states and private insurance companies designed to encourage individuals to plan for their long-term care needs while reducing potential Medicaid expenditures.

How Partnership Programs Work:

When you purchase a qualifying long-term care insurance policy, you receive dollar-for-dollar asset protection equal to the benefits paid out by your policy.

If you exhaust your policy benefits and need to apply for Medicaid, you can protect assets equal to what your policy paid out from Medicaid spend-down requirements.

For example, if your partnership policy paid $300,000 in benefits, you could protect $300,000 in assets while still qualifying for Medicaid.

Key Benefits:

- Provides incentive to purchase private long-term care insurance

- Offers a safety net if care needs extend beyond policy benefits
- Allows preservation of some assets for spouses or heirs
- Reduces potential Medicaid costs by encouraging private coverage first

Availability and Requirements:

- Not all states participate in Partnership Programs
- Policies must meet specific requirements to qualify
- Benefits vary by state

Partnership Programs offer a middle ground between complete self-reliance and full dependence on government programs, making them an important consideration in comprehensive long-term care planning.

VETERANS BENEFITS: LIMITED SUPPORT FOR THOSE WHO SERVED

Veterans who served during wartime periods may qualify for the Department of Veterans Affairs (VA) Aid and Attendance benefit, which provides monthly payments to help cover the cost of long-term care.

Eligibility and Benefits

To qualify, veterans must have served at least 90 days of active duty, with at least one day during a wartime period. They must have received a discharge other than dishonorable and meet specific medical and financial need criteria.

The medical requirement involves needing assistance with activities of daily living, being bedridden, residing in a nursing home, or having severe visual impairment.[53]

For 2026, eligible veterans can receive monthly Aid and Attendance benefits ranging from approximately $1,558 (surviving spouse) to $2,874 (married veteran), with the specific amount determined by their marital status and required level of care. In cases where both spouses are veterans who qualify, the benefit can reach $3,845 monthly.

While these benefits supplement the broader VA Pension program and can help offset expenses for home care, assisted living, or nursing facility services, they typically cover only a portion of the total cost in most care settings.[54]

VA benefits do come with several limitations. The application process can be lengthy, often taking 3-9 months from submission to approval, depending on complexity and VA backlogs. Financial eligibility requirements, while less stringent than Medicaid, still limit assets and income.

Recent rule changes have implemented a three-year lookback period similar to Medicaid's five-year period.

For veterans with service-connected disabilities, additional VA benefits may be available, including access to VA nursing homes and more comprehensive home care services. These benefits are generally more robust than the Aid and Attendance program but are limited to those whose care needs stem directly from service-related conditions.

 **NAVIGATOR STORY**

DENNIS

Dennis, a 78-year-old Vietnam War veteran, watched as his wife's osteo-arthritis gradually worsened over the years. What began as occasional joint pain had progressed to severe mobility limitations requiring daily assistance.

"When Barbara could no longer climb the stairs or dress herself, we knew we needed help," Dennis explains. "Her doctor confirmed the severe progression of her osteoarthritis, and we started with part-time care that quickly became full-time."

Dennis applied for VA Aid and Attendance benefits, but the process proved challenging. "The paperwork was overwhelming, and it took over seven months to get approved. By then, we had already spent a significant amount on home care aides."

When approval finally came, the monthly benefit of $2,642 helped but fell far short of covering their $6,200 monthly home care expenses. While grateful for the assistance, Dennis had to continue drawing down their savings at a rate that concerned him deeply.

"The VA benefit has been helpful, but it's not the complete solution we'd hoped for," he says. "I wish we'd understood earlier that we needed a more comprehensive plan for Barbara's progressive condition."

THE PROGRAM OF ALL-INCLUSIVE CARE FOR THE ELDERLY (PACE)

PACE is a lesser known but valuable program that provides com-prehensive medical and social services to certain frail, elderly individuals who qualify for nursing home care but wish to remain in their communities. This innovative model integrates Medicare and Medicaid funding to provide coordinated care through an interdisciplinary team approach.

To qualify for PACE, individuals must be 55 or older, live in a PACE service area, meet their state's criteria for nursing home level of care, and be able to live safely in the community with PACE support.[55]

PACE programs typically offer a comprehensive range of services including adult day care, medical care, home health care, prescription drugs, and social services.

While PACE offers comprehensive services, it has significant limitations. The program is available in limited geographic areas, with many states having few or no PACE programs.

As of August 2025, over 85,000 individuals were enrolled in PACE programs nationwide, a tiny fraction of those needing long-term care.[56] Participants must use PACE physicians and providers, surrendering some choice in their healthcare decisions.

THE REALITY OF GOVERNMENT PROGRAMS: A FRAGMENTED SYSTEM

When viewed collectively, government programs for long-term care reveal a fragmented system with significant gaps:

- **Medicare** provides excellent acute care coverage but minimal long-term care support.

- **Medicaid** offers comprehensive coverage, but only after impoverishment—and even then, many applicants face wait lists for home and community-based services or limited access to preferred facilities.

- **VA Benefits** provide supplemental support for a limited population.

- **Partnership Programs** bridge private insurance and Medicaid, allowing middle-class individuals to protect assets equal to their insurance benefits, but are limited to traditional LTC policies and unavailable in several states.

- **PACE** offers innovative community-based care but with limited availability.

This patchwork of programs leaves many middle-income Americans in a precarious position—too wealthy to qualify for government assistance but unable to afford the full cost of long-term care without depleting their life savings.

The "middle market" gap represents one of the most significant challenges in extended care financing.

Several factors contribute to this fragmented approach. Extended care has historically fallen between healthcare and social services, with neither system taking full responsibility.

Budget constraints at both federal and state levels have limited program expansion. Additionally, the complexity of long-term care needs makes standardized solutions difficult to implement effectively.

> **BOTTOM LINE:** Government programs for long-term care represent a fragmented system with significant eligibility restrictions and coverage limitations. They should be viewed as a backstop rather than a primary funding strategy for most Americans.

PLANNING IMPLICATIONS: BEYOND THE GOVERNMENT SAFETY NET

Understanding the limitations of government programs leads to several important planning implications.

First, government programs should be viewed as a safety net of last resort, not as a primary funding strategy for extended care. Relying solely on these programs typically means accepting significant limitations in choice, quality, and setting.

Proactive planning becomes essential given the significant gaps in government coverage. Creating a personal long-term care plan while options remain available provides greater control and flexibility than waiting until care is needed, and choices are limited.

For those who may eventually rely on government programs, understanding eligibility requirements and planning accordingly can help preserve some assets while ensuring access to needed care. This coordination strategy requires careful navigation of complex rules, typically with professional guidance.

The limitations of current programs highlight the need for broader policy solutions to address the growing long-term care needs of an aging population.

As America's population ages, pressure on existing systems will intensify, potentially leading to policy changes that could affect planning strategies.

For most Americans, a sound extended care strategy will involve some combination of personal resources, family support, and private funding options, with government programs serving as a backstop rather than a primary funding source.

This layered approach provides the greatest flexibility and protection against the limitations of any single funding mechanism.

NAVIGATING THE SYSTEM: ADVOCACY AND ASSISTANCE

Despite their limitations, government programs remain an important component of the long-term care landscape, particularly for those with limited resources.

Navigating these complex systems often requires specialized knowledge and persistent advocacy. Several resources can provide valuable assistance. State Health Insurance Assistance Programs (SHIPs) offer free counseling and assistance with Medicare questions, including coverage for skilled nursing care (shiphelp.org).

National Association of Area Agencies on Aging provide information about local resources, including Medicaid waiver programs and other community-based services (n4a.org or eldercare.acl.gov).

For veterans, Veterans Service Organizations (VSOs) offer assistance with VA benefit applications, often significantly improving approval rates and reducing processing times (va.gov).

Elder law attorneys specialize in issues affecting seniors, including Medicaid planning and appeals. Their expertise can be particularly valuable when dealing with complex eligibility questions or developing strategies to protect assets while qualifying for benefits (naela.org).

LOOKING AHEAD: POLICY TRENDS AND POTENTIAL CHANGES

The long-term care landscape continues to evolve as policymakers grapple with the challenges of an aging population and rising care costs.

Medicare Advantage plans are increasingly offering limited long-term care benefits, potentially signaling a gradual expansion of Medicare's role in long-term care.

Medicaid programs in many states are shifting toward home and community-based services rather than institutional care.

Various policy proposals for addressing the extended care financing challenge have emerged, including catastrophic coverage programs, tax incentives for private insurance, and social insurance approaches similar to those implemented in other countries.

Technology is enabling new care delivery models that may influence government program design, potentially reducing reliance on institutional settings.

For planning purposes, it's prudent to base decisions on current program structures while remaining aware of potential changes.

The fundamental limitations of government programs—particularly their means-tested nature and focus on basic rather than comprehensive care—are likely to persist even as specific features evolve.

All worksheets and templates for this book are online at
WWW.YOURRETIREMENTBLINDSPOT.COM/RESOURCES
Complete them as digital forms or download PDFs. Scan the QR code here:

———

1. Review the Medicare & Long-Term Care Worksheet to understand specific coverage limitations.

2. Research your state's specific Medicaid eligibility requirements and coverage options.

3. If applicable, determine your potential eligibility for veterans' benefits.

4. Identify local resources such as your Area Agency on Aging and State Health Insurance Assistance Program.

5. Consider consulting with an elder law attorney to understand how government programs might fit into your overall long-term care plan.

INSURANCE SOLUTIONS FOR LONG-TERM CARE

- Long-term care insurance has evolved from nursing-home-only coverage to comprehensive options

- Today's market offers both traditional policies and hybrid solutions

- Short-term care insurance provides limited duration benefits with simpler underwriting for those who may not qualify for traditional coverage

- Life insurance policies with acceleration riders provide limited long-term care benefits while primarily serving as life insurance

- Key policy features include benefit amount, duration, inflation protection, and payment method

- Cash indemnity policies may offer more flexibility than reimbursement models

- Both traditional and hybrid policies may offer tax advantages

THE EVOLUTION OF LONG-TERM CARE INSURANCE

Long-term care insurance has been around since the mid-1970s, but the product you can buy today barely resembles what your parents might have considered. Understanding why the market evolved—and what nearly broke it—is essential context for making informed decisions about your own protection.

The earliest long-term care policies were primarily nursing home-only coverage with limited benefits and numerous exclusions. By the 1990s, the market had expanded dramatically, with policies offering comprehensive coverage across multiple care settings.

However, the early 2000s brought challenges as insurers faced claims experience that exceeded projections, historically low interest rates that affected investment returns, and lower-than-expected policy lapse rates.

These challenges forced the industry to evolve or die. The result? A more disciplined marketplace with sustainable products—but also higher barriers to entry and less room for complacency. These factors led to substantial changes:

- Several major carriers exited the traditional long-term care insurance business

- Remaining carriers implemented significant premium increases on existing policies

- New policies featured more conservative pricing, stricter underwriting, and modified benefit designs to ensure sustainability

Today's long-term care insurance landscape has adapted to address past failures and consumer concerns. The market now offers two primary approaches—traditional long-term care insurance and hybrid (asset-based or policy-linked) solutions—along with alternative options like short-term care insurance and life insurance with acceleration riders.

Each approach has unique characteristics, advantages, and considerations that must be carefully evaluated based on individual circumstances and preferences. Understanding their distinct features is critical to designing the right strategy for your situation.

TRADITIONAL LONG-TERM CARE INSURANCE: STRUCTURE AND BENEFITS

Traditional long-term care insurance is a pure insurance product, meaning it's designed specifically to cover long-term care costs without the life insurance or annuity components found in hybrid alternatives. These policies are tax-qualified under IRC §7702B, which provides important consumer protections and ensures that benefits received for qualifying long-term care expenses are generally tax-free.

KEY POINT: Traditional long-term care insurance typically provides more benefit per premium dollar than other solutions when care is needed. While often described as "use it or lose it," some policies now offer optional return of premium riders that can refund premiums under specific circumstances.

This focused approach offers several advantages, including lower initial outlay compared to hybrid alternatives, the ability to customize coverage to specific needs and budget, and greater leverage—providing more benefit per premium dollar if care is needed. Many policies offer couples discounts and shared benefit options while maintaining tax-qualified status, allowing potential tax deductions for premiums.

How Traditional Policies Work

Benefits typically become available when the insured cannot perform two of six activities of daily living (transferring, toileting, bathing, dressing, eating and continence) or has a severe cognitive impairment requiring substantial supervision.

Most policies include a waiting period, called an elimination period, before benefits are payable (commonly 0, 30, 60, 90, or 180 days; some carriers offer longer, and options vary by state). It works like a time-based deductible: you cover costs during that time.

Policies specify a daily or monthly benefit amount—the maximum the policy will pay for covered services. Most policies offer a choice of daily benefit amounts, typically from $100 to $500 per day or monthly equivalents. They also define how long benefits will be paid—two to five years are common; lifetime options are also available from select carriers.

Inflation protection increases benefits over time to help keep pace with rising care costs. Common options include 3% simple, 3% compound, or 5% compound annual increases.

Coverage and Services

Today's traditional long-term care policies typically cover care across multiple settings, including the insured's home, adult day care centers, assisted living facilities and nursing homes.

Most policies include care coordination services, caregiver training, respite care, and bed reservation benefits. Some offer a blended payment approach such as 25% available as a cash benefit, with the remainder paid as reimbursement by submitting receipts.

Underwriting and Premium Considerations

When you apply for traditional long-term care insurance, the carrier will evaluate your health and typically place you in one of four categories: Preferred, Standard, Class I, or Class II.

Those in excellent health qualify for Preferred rates, the lowest premiums with full access to all benefit options. Standard applicants are in good health but may have some minor health concerns; they pay moderate premiums, higher than Preferred but lower than Class I, while still maintaining access to a wide range of benefits.

Class I applicants have more noticeable health concerns and pay higher premiums with somewhat limited policy options. Class II applicants have significant health issues, resulting in the highest premiums and potentially more limited policy options.

Underwriting standards vary by insurer, and while the process is thorough, many applicants with managed health conditions can still qualify for coverage. Most policies are designed with long-term premium structures, though various payment options may be available depending on the carrier and product.

A valuable feature of most traditional policies is the waiver of premium benefit. This consumer-friendly provision means that once you begin receiving covered care and complete your elimination period, you no longer need to pay premiums while receiving benefits. This provides significant financial relief during a time when you're facing substantial care expenses. Your premium obligations only resume if you recover from your condition and no longer require care.

Advantages and Limitations

While often characterized as "use it or lose it" insurance, some policies now offer return of premium riders that can refund premiums under certain circumstances, such as death before age 65 or return of premium less claims paid.

However, these policies also have limitations. Generally, premiums are not guaranteed and may increase over time. There is no death benefit available, and without optional return of premium riders, no benefits are provided if care is never needed.

NAVIGATOR STORY

XAVIER & CEDRICA

Xavier and Cedrica, both 58, wanted a focused way to protect their retirement from extended care costs without overbuying life insurance. With $1.2 million earmarked for retirement, they weren't interested in hoping markets and health would cooperate.

Their advisor recommended traditional long-term care insurance. After underwriting, they each secured their own policy with coordinated features for control and flexibility.

For a combined lifetime premium of $452 per month (about $5,424 annually), each policy provides a $3,000 monthly benefit with a five-year benefit period—creating individual pools of $180,000 each. Home Care and Adult Day Care start immediately with a zero-day elimination period, while facility care follows a 90-day elimination period.

They added a 15% cash benefit option, available in addition to full monthly reimbursement, so each can receive up to $450 per month without submitting receipts while other eligible care is still reimbursed. A 3% compound inflation rider helps benefits keep pace over time.

They also elected a Shared Care rider: if one spouse exhausts their pool, they can access the other spouse's remaining benefits, subject to policy terms.

"What convinced us was how it actually works when life gets messy," Cedrica says. "Care at home can start right away, we can use some cash for family help or incidentals, and the inflation rider keeps our buying power from eroding."

Xavier adds, "We each have our own $180,000 pool, same coverage terms, and if care is at home or assisted living, the full monthly amount is available, no reduction. That clarity matters."

"Traditional long-term care insurance was the right fit for us," Cedrica concludes. "We already had life insurance, so we preferred a solution with manageable premiums that focuses specifically on what concerns us most—protecting our retirement from care costs."

This hypothetical example is based on a sample illustration for a 58-year-old couple using traditional long-term care insurance. Actual benefits, premiums, features, and policy availability vary by product, carrier, state, age, health, and underwriting class. Approval is subject to underwriting and product availability. Premiums are not guaranteed and may increase in the future on a class basis. Benefits are subject to eligibility requirements, elimination periods, exclusions, limitations, and policy terms; the governing contract controls. The amounts shown are illustrative only and not guaranteed. This material is for informational purposes and is not an offer, solicitation, or recommendation. Consult a licensed insurance professional for personalized illustrations and an Outline of Coverage; review all policy terms carefully. Tax treatment depends on individual circumstances; consult your tax advisor.

HYBRID LONG-TERM CARE SOLUTIONS: THE MULTI-BENEFIT STRATEGY

Hybrid long-term care products (also known as asset-based or policy-linked) solve the single biggest objection to traditional coverage: the fear that if you never need care, your premiums are gone forever. These products combine long-term care benefits with either life insurance or an annuity, ensuring that whether you need care or not, value flows either to you or your beneficiaries.

This guarantee has fueled their explosive growth. Hybrid policies now represent a significant and growing segment of the long-term care insurance market, appealing to those who want protection without the "use it or lose it" risk.

Life Insurance-Based Hybrid Policies

True hybrid long-term care policies built on life insurance are qualified under tax code IRC §7702B. This means the benefits you receive for care are generally tax-free, your premiums are guaranteed and won't increase, and you have specific consumer protections built in.

These policies provide a death benefit that can be accessed for long-term care expenses. If you never need care, the full death benefit passes to your beneficiaries tax-free. This distinguishes them fundamentally from regular life insurance with accelerated benefit riders, which don't qualify as true long-term care insurance and don't offer the same tax advantages or guarantees.

True hybrid policies feature guaranteed premiums that cannot increase, providing financial predictability that many clients value. You can choose from flexible payment options, including single-premium payments or limited-pay structures over 5, 7, 10, or 15 years, or even pay to age 65, 95, or 100. If you never need care, your beneficiaries receive the death benefit tax-free, eliminating the "use it or lose it" concern of traditional policies.

Many hybrid policies offer extension of benefit riders that provide care benefits beyond the policy's death benefit, with some offering lifetime benefit options. Most products include return of premium options, giving you additional flexibility. These policies provide a leverage factor, delivering multiple times your premium in long-term care benefits, with younger applicants typically receiving higher multiples than those purchasing in their 70s.

For those with existing life insurance policies, 1035 exchange opportunities allow tax-free transfers into these hybrid solutions. Some products offer simplified underwriting with fewer health questions, though underwriting standards remain thorough to ensure proper risk assessment.

Annuity-Based Hybrid Policies

Annuity-based long-term care solutions are specialized annuity contracts that incorporate built-in long-term care benefits. These products provide dedicated, contractually guaranteed long-term care coverage—typically offering a pool of benefits that is a multiple of your annuity's account value when you meet qualifying care requirements.

> **KEY POINT:** Hybrid policies transform what could be viewed as an expense (traditional long-term care insurance) into an asset that provides multiple benefits - protecting against long-term care costs while preserving wealth for your legacy goals.

These annuity-based solutions are typically funded with a single premium payment, making them straightforward for consumers who prefer a one-time investment. If long-term care is never needed, the account value passes to your beneficiaries as a death benefit, ensuring that your investment is not lost. Additionally, you maintain access to your annuity value subject to applicable surrender schedules, providing both potential liquidity during your lifetime and legacy protection.

The Pension Protection Act of 2006 (PPA) provides significant tax advantages for these products, allowing benefits paid for long-term care to be received tax-free. (See the Tax Advantages section later in this chapter for full details.)

Many annuity-based hybrid policies feature simplified underwriting with less stringent health qualifications, often requiring only a few targeted health questions. This makes them more accessible to a wider range of individuals, particularly those who may have difficulty qualifying for traditional LTC insurance or life-based hybrid solutions. Some products offer joint coverage options, allowing couples to share benefits.

Important Distinction: While annuity-based hybrid solutions offer valuable benefits, they typically do not provide the same leverage potential (benefit per premium dollar) as hybrid policies with a life insurance chassis. This means that for the same premium amount, you may receive a smaller benefit pool compared to a life-based hybrid solution.

However, hybrid policies also have limitations. They typically require a higher initial premium compared to traditional LTC insurance. Some hybrid products offer more limited inflation protection options compared to traditional policies, and there's an opportunity cost of committing assets that could otherwise be invested differently. Additionally, while hybrid policies provide valuable protection, they may offer less leverage (benefit per premium dollar) than traditional LTC insurance policies, which are designed specifically as pure insurance products rather than serving multiple purposes.

BOTTOM LINE: Asset-based (hybrid) long-term care solutions address the "use it or lose it" concern of traditional insurance. Whether built on life insurance or annuity platforms, these products provide substantial benefits for care if needed, while preserving value for beneficiaries if care is never required, offering both protection and peace of mind.

 **NAVIGATOR STORY**

WEI & JIA

Wei and Jia, both 62, were considering long-term care insurance but were concerned about investing in premiums for coverage they might never need. Their financial advisor suggested a hybrid long-term care policy with a shared pool of benefits for both spouses.

"What appealed to us was the certainty," Jia explains. "We repositioned $150,000 from our conservative investments into a policy that provides $450,000 of long-term care benefits for 8 years, growing with inflation. If we never need care, our children receive at least $150,000 tax-free when we pass away."

The couple appreciates that they've simultaneously addressed the need for long-term care protection, return of premium, and a guaranteed death benefit if care isn't needed.

"We sleep better knowing we have protection against what could be our biggest retirement expense," Wei says. "And we don't worry about throwing money away on something we might never use."

This hypothetical example is based on a sample illustration for a 62-year-old couple using a hybrid long-term care insurance policy. The policy provides a shared pool of benefits for both spouses. Actual benefits, premiums, and guarantees will vary by product, carrier, age, health status, inflation protection elected, and state availability. Benefit amounts shown are for illustrative purposes only and are not guaranteed. Guarantees are based on the claims-paying ability of the issuing insurance company. This example is for illustrative purposes only and does not constitute a recommendation or offer of insurance. Please consult a licensed insurance professional for personalized illustrations and product details.

CASH INDEMNITY VS. REIMBURSEMENT MODELS

An important distinction among long-term care policies is how benefits are paid—either through a reimbursement model or a cash indemnity approach. This difference fundamentally affects how benefits can be used and the flexibility available to policyholders when care is needed.

- **Reimbursement Model:** With reimbursement policies, the insured submits bills and receipts for qualifying care expenses, and the insurance company reimburses up to the policy's maximum benefit. Benefits are paid only for covered services actually received, typically from licensed providers, and any unused portion of the monthly benefit is not paid to the insured. The availability of direct billing can be very convenient, allowing claims and payments to flow directly to care providers and reducing the administrative burden on the insured. Most traditional long-term care policies and many hybrid products use the reimbursement model.

- **Cash Indemnity Model:** With cash indemnity policies, once benefit triggers are met, the full daily or monthly benefit is paid directly to the policyholder—no receipts are required after initial qualification. The insured generally has broad flexibility in how benefits are used, including paying family members for care, covering informal care, or making home modifications; tax limits may apply if benefits exceed qualified expenses. A handful of hybrid products and some traditional policies offer partial cash indemnity benefits; these designs may be priced higher or provide lower benefit amounts for the same premium than reimbursement models, though results vary by carrier and state.

- **Combination Models:** Some policies combine both approaches, offering a portion of the benefit as cash indemnity and the remainder as reimbursement within the same policy. This combination structure provides added flexibility while helping manage premium costs.

> **BOTTOM LINE:** The choice between reimbursement and cash indemnity models is a personal preference based on your specific situation, anticipated care needs, and budget considerations. Neither approach is inherently better—the right choice depends on how you value cost efficiency versus flexibility in your long-term care planning.

SHORT-TERM CARE INSURANCE: A LIMITED DURATION OPTION

Short-term care insurance provides benefits for a limited period—typically 90, 180, or 365 days—to help cover the costs of qualifying care services. These policies emerged as an alternative for individuals seeking more affordable coverage or those who may not qualify for traditional long-term care insurance due to age or health conditions.

Coverage extends to home health care, assisted living facilities, and nursing home care, similar to traditional long-term care insurance but for shorter durations. Key features include generally lower premiums, many policies with no elimination period allowing benefits to begin day one, less stringent underwriting requirements making coverage accessible to older adults, simplified application processes with fewer health questions, guaranteed renewability if premiums are paid, and daily or monthly benefits selected to match local costs.

These policies offer accessible coverage for older adults or those with health conditions that might disqualify them from traditional long-term care insurance, lower premiums making coverage more affordable, and immediate benefits with no elimination period in many policies.

These policies can be useful to cover short recovery windows or bridge gaps during a traditional or hybrid long-term care policy's elimination period.

However, these policies also have limitations, including the obvious constraint of covering only short-term care needs with benefits typically lasting a maximum of one year. They may not be available in all states due to varying regulatory requirements, and they generally do not offer inflation protection, meaning the benefit amount remains fixed throughout the life of the policy.

BOTTOM LINE: Short-term care insurance offers targeted, time-limited coverage at lower premiums with simplified underwriting, making it valuable for bridging care gaps or serving those unable to qualify for traditional or hybrid long-term care insurance.

LIFE INSURANCE WITH ACCELERATION RIDERS

In addition to traditional and hybrid long-term care insurance, life insurance policies with acceleration riders have emerged as another option in the extended care planning landscape. These products allow policyholders to access a portion of their death benefit early if they meet certain health-related conditions.

Several types of acceleration riders exist, each serving different needs:

- **Chronic illness riders** allow access to death benefits if the insured develops a qualifying chronic illness, typically defined as being unable to perform two of six activities of daily living (ADLs) or having severe cognitive impairment.. Most chronic illness riders are governed by IRC Section 101(g) and traditionally required the condition to be expected to be permanent; some newer products have relaxed that requirement, so contract language matters.[57]

- **True long-term care (LTC) riders**, less common but available on some policies, are tax-qualified under IRC Section 7702B. These generally do not require the condition to be permanent and offer broader consumer protections, though they may have additional underwriting requirements.[58]

- **Critical illness riders** provide benefits upon diagnosis of specified serious conditions such as cancer, heart attack, or stroke, regardless of whether long-term care is needed.

- **Terminal illness riders** (typically included in most modern policies) allow access to death benefits for those diagnosed with a terminal condition and limited life expectancy.

> **KEY POINT:** Life Insurance with Acceleration Riders add practical flexibility—money you can access while living if qualifying health conditions occur. Not a substitute for qualified long-term care policies. Review how benefits trigger, pay, and reduce death benefits.

When a policyholder activates an acceleration rider, benefits are typically paid as a lump sum or periodic acceleration. This reduces the death benefit dollar-for-dollar, though some riders calculate a discounted amount at claim, depending on the design. Some chronic illness riders are included at no additional premium, while others have explicit charges.

Life insurance with acceleration riders provides dual protection—life insurance plus potential access to funds for health conditions. If care is never needed, the death benefit remains intact (assuming the policy stays in force and no accelerations are taken). These products generally have a simpler structure than hybrid products and different underwriting requirements than both hybrid and traditional long-term care insurance, though eligibility still depends on age and health.

> **BOTTOM LINE:** Life insurance with acceleration riders can provide limited long-term care protection, but is primarily designed as life insurance. This approach may appeal to those seeking simplified coverage or an alternative to traditional long-term care insurance, but eligibility and benefits vary by product and by state.

However, these products have important limitations compared to dedicated long-term care solutions. Most riders lack comprehensive benefit structures, including limited or no inflation protection, fixed acceleration percentages rather than flexible benefit amounts, less coverage for home care services, and absence of care coordination services.

Additionally, they are typically not LTC insurance and do not include the full LTC consumer protections of §7702B.

NAVIGATOR STORY

DANIEL

Daniel, 56, purchased a permanent life insurance policy with a chronic illness rider included at no added upfront premium primarily to provide financial protection for his wife and children. Five years later, he was diagnosed with multiple sclerosis (MS).

"Initially, I thought I'd be able to tap into my life insurance through the rider," Daniel explains. "But I discovered two important limitations. First, in the early stages my condition wasn't certified as 'expected to be permanent' under the rider language—my doctor wouldn't attest that I'd never recover. Second, once I did qualify years later, using the rider significantly reduced the death benefit I had intended for my family."

While Daniel eventually accessed benefits under the rider, he found them less predictable than he expected, particularly for the home care he preferred, discounted at claim and not structured like dedicated long-term care benefits. "The rider provided some help, but I wish I'd understood the difference between it and true long-term care coverage," he reflects. "If long-term care protection had been my primary goal rather than life insurance, I would have chosen differently."

DESIGNING THE RIGHT COVERAGE: KEY DECISIONS

Creating appropriate long-term care coverage involves several important decisions that should be carefully considered based on individual circumstances, preferences, and financial resources.

When determining your daily or monthly benefit amount, consider current care costs in your preferred location and how much you can comfortably co-fund from other income sources.

The U.S. Department of Health and Human Services notes that most people will need some form of long-term care, and the costs can be significant.[59] Many advisors suggest covering a substantial portion of anticipated expenses with insurance, balancing premium costs with meaningful protection. The ideal benefit period balances coverage adequacy with premium affordability.

KEY POINT: Without inflation protection, your benefits will not keep pace with rising care costs. A $150 daily benefit that seems adequate today could cover less than half of the actual cost when you need care 20-30 years in the future.

About two-thirds of today's 65-year-olds will need some type of long-term care during their remaining years. Women need care longer (3.7 years) than men (2.2 years). Most care will be provided at home by unpaid family members and friends.[60]

Cognitive conditions like Alzheimer's disease often require longer care periods, and family health history may suggest longer or shorter care needs. While lifetime benefits provide maximum protection, they may come at an increased premium cost.

Without inflation protection, a policy's benefits will lose purchasing power over time. Long-term care costs have historically increased at 3-5% annually. The longer the period between purchase and potential claim, the more important inflation protection becomes.

Compound inflation protection provides significantly more benefit than simple inflation over longer periods. For those under 65, compound inflation protection (3% or 5%) is typically recommended. Those over 70 might consider simple inflation or a larger initial benefit with more modest inflation protection.

Many policies offer couples the ability to share benefits between spouses or partners. This approach creates a larger pool of benefits accessible to either person, addresses the reality that care needs often differ between spouses, and typically provides more efficient coverage than two completely separate policies.

Even with single policies, couples often qualify for significant discounts when both partners apply, typically in the range of 30%. Some policies maintain this discount even if one spouse later passes away.

The elimination period represents the number of days the insured must pay for care before benefits begin. Longer elimination periods reduce premiums but typically increase out-of-pocket costs when care is needed. Most policies offer 30, 60, 90, or 180-day options, with 90 days being the most common choice.

TAX ADVANTAGES OF LONG-TERM CARE INSURANCE

Both traditional and hybrid long-term care insurance can provide tax benefits. Understanding these advantages is essential when evaluating your coverage options.

For traditional long-term care insurance, premiums may be deductible as medical expenses if you itemize deductions and your total medical expenses exceed 7.5% of your adjusted gross income. The deductible amount is subject to annual IRS limits based on your age.[61]

In the case of hybrid long-term care policies, only the portion of the premium that specifically covers long-term care may be deductible. This deduction is contingent upon the insurance company providing the necessary information regarding the deductible amount, and it is also subject to age-based limits and other IRS regulations.

Regardless of how premiums are paid, benefits received from a qualified long-term care insurance policy are generally tax-free.[62]

Death benefits from hybrid policies are typically received income tax-free by beneficiaries.[63]

The Pension Protection Act of 2006 allows for 1035 exchanges, enabling individuals to transfer funds from an existing life insurance or annuity contract into a hybrid long-term care policy. This can provide additional tax advantages, as the transferred funds can continue to grow tax-deferred and be used for long-term care benefits tax-free.

Self-employed individuals and business owners have additional opportunities for tax deductions. They can deduct premiums paid for long-term care insurance as a business expense, including coverage set up for employees. Business owners can also implement executive bonus arrangements for key employees or create carve-out plans for specific employee groups.[64] (See Chapter 12 for comprehensive coverage of tax strategies for business owners.)

Consulting with a qualified tax professional is essential to understand the specific tax implications for your situation. The information provided here is general in nature and should not be considered tax advice.

> **BOTTOM LINE:** Both traditional and hybrid long-term care policies offer meaningful tax advantages: potential premium deductibility (age-based limits apply), generally tax-free qualified benefits, and—uniquely for hybrids—1035 exchanges and income tax-free death benefits for beneficiaries. Business owners and the self-employed may access additional deductions under corporate and self-employed rules. Always coordinate with a tax professional.

THE UNDERWRITING PROCESS: PREPARING FOR SUCCESS

Underwriting for long-term care coverage is typically more stringent than for life insurance, as insurers assess not just mortality risk but morbidity risk—the likelihood of chronic illness or disability.

Understanding this process can help improve your chances of approval and favorable rates.

The underwriting process usually includes a detailed health questionnaire, review of medical records, and a personal health interview, often conducted by telephone, and sometimes face-to-face. Cognitive assessments are common for applicants over age 65 and older, and some cases may require lab tests or a brief medical exam.

Some hybrid products utilize simplified or limited under-writing, particularly in group or special-offer settings. However, most individual comprehensive long-term care solutions are fully underwritten and necessitate a thorough review of the applicant's health history. This is crucial as the underwriting process is designed to evaluate the risk associated with insuring an individual based on their health background and lifestyle choices.

Underwriters typically evaluate conditions such as mobility limitations requiring assistive devices, recent or scheduled hospitalizations or surgeries, pending medical procedures, ongoing physical therapy, neurological conditions, diabetes with complications, history of stroke or TIA (mini stroke), memory or cognitive concerns, history of multiple falls, and obesity when combined with other health factors. Understanding what underwriters look for can help you prepare a stronger application and set realistic expectations.

To improve your underwriting outcome, apply while in good health, provide complete and accurate information, address controllable health factors before applying. Working with an experienced insurance professional can also be beneficial, as they can help match your health profile with the right carriers and pre-screen your case to identify potential issues before submission.

 **NAVIGATOR STORY**

NICK & KIKI

Nick and Kiki, both 58, decided to explore long-term care insurance after observing the challenges and complexities associated with Kiki's mother's prolonged experience with Alzheimer's disease.

"I thought it would be similar to when we got life insurance years ago," Nick explains. "But the health questions were much more detailed, covering everything from prescription medications to our parents' health history to whether we'd had any falls or balance issues."

Kiki was initially declined by their first-choice company due to a combination of osteopenia (early bone loss) and a recent wrist fracture from a fall. Their certified long-term care specialist then recommended a different carrier with more favorable underwriting criteria for Kiki's specific situation.

"We're so glad we worked with someone who knew the differences between companies," Kiki says. "The second company approved me at standard rates, even though the first declined me entirely."

Their experience highlights the importance of applying while still in generally good health and working with an experienced professional who understands each carrier's underwriting preferences."

MAKING THE RIGHT CHOICE: COMPARING ALL OPTIONS

The choice among traditional long-term care insurance, hybrid solutions, short-term care insurance, and life insurance with accelerated benefit riders depends on individual circumstances, preferences, and priorities. Each approach offers distinct advantages and considerations that should be carefully evaluated.

- **Traditional long-term care insurance** fits those who seek maximum leverage (benefit per premium dollar) for long-term care, can tolerate the possibility of future premium increases, and are primarily concerned with long-term care protection rather than a death benefit.

- **Hybrid solutions** fit those who are concerned about the "use it or lose it" aspect of traditional LTC insurance, want guaranteed premiums, have existing assets that can be repositioned or prefer to pay premiums over time, desire legacy benefits for heirs if care isn't needed, have specific estate planning or wealth transfer objectives, and prefer simplified or alternative underwriting options (more common with annuity-based designs; varies by carrier and state).

- **Short-term care insurance** fits those who are older or have health conditions that might prevent qualifying for traditional long-term care insurance, seek more affordable premiums with immediate coverage (no elimination period), need coverage for a limited duration (for example, to bridge the gap during a traditional or hybrid policy's elimination period), or are looking for simpler underwriting and application processes.

- **Life insurance with accelerated benefit riders** fits those who need life insurance coverage as their primary goal, want some protection against long-term care needs as a secondary benefit, have a limited budget that cannot accommodate dedicated long-term care coverage, are primarily concerned with providing for beneficiaries but want added flexibility, and are comfortable with the rider's eligibility rules and potential discounting of benefits at claim rather than dollar-for-dollar accelerations.

Some financial and insurance professionals might recommend a blended approach for certain clients. This could include using short-term long-term care combined with a traditional policy with a longer elimination period, or ensuring adequate life insurance with riders while adding a smaller amount of dedicated long-term care protection with a traditional long-term care policy.

> **BOTTOM LINE:** The right solution depends on your planning objectives. Traditional long-term care offers comprehensive coverage for long-term care needs. Short-term care provides more accessible protection for limited durations. Life insurance with riders prioritizes death benefits with secondary care protection. Hybrid solutions balance care benefits and legacy planning.

THE FUTURE OF LONG-TERM CARE INSURANCE

The long-term care insurance market continues to evolve in response to consumer preferences, claims experience, and economic factors. Emerging trends include increased focus on wellness programs and preventive services, more flexible benefit designs that adapt to changing care delivery models, integration with other financial products and services, technology-enabled care coordination and claims processing, and new underwriting approaches using predictive analytics and alternative data sources.

One notable example of this evolution is Bridge®, a fixed index annuity (FIA) with a 7702B long-term care rider offered by EquiTrust. This guaranteed issue hybrid annuity solution addresses a critical gap in the market by offering:

- **Guaranteed issue** — Everyone is approved, *making coverage accessible to those with health conditions who cannot qualify for traditional or standard hybrid policies*

- **Index annuity growth potential** — Cash value tied to market index performance with downside protection, providing potential growth while preserving principal

- **7702B tax-qualified LTC benefits** — Tax-free withdrawals for qualified long-term care expenses, delivering the same tax advantages as dedicated LTC insurance policies

This type of solution represents a significant shift in accessibility, particularly for individuals in their 60s and 70s who face health-based declines or have been previously declined for coverage.

Note: Product features, availability, and terms are subject to change and may not be available in all states. Consult a qualified long-term care specialist for current details.

What This Evolution Means for You

The expansion of guaranteed issue options is good news. It means more people have access to tax-qualified long-term care protection, even when traditional underwriting would decline them. But here's the reality: your health directly impacts the leverage you can create.

Medically underwritten policies typically offer significantly higher benefit multiples for the same premium dollar. Guaranteed issue products provide critical access when health is an obstacle, but they deliver less leverage than what's available when you qualify medically.

Your health is an asset. While the door remains open for coverage through guaranteed issue solutions, the most efficient planning happens while you can still qualify for maximum leverage. Waiting doesn't eliminate options. It reduces efficiency.

The most successful extended care planning strategies involve a combination of approaches tailored to individual circumstances and preferences. By understanding the full range of available options and working with experienced professionals, you can create comprehensive plans that protect both your assets and your families from the potential impact of extended care needs.

BOTTOM LINE: There is no one-size-fits-all solution for long-term care planning. The right approach depends on your health, finances, family situation, and personal preferences. Working with a qualified insurance professional or financial advisor who understands the full range of options is essential for creating an optimal strategy—and doing it while you still have the health and time to secure the coverage you need.

☑ ACTION STEPS CHECKLIST

All worksheets and templates for this book are online at
WWW.YOURRETIREMENTBLINDSPOT.COM/RESOURCES
Complete them as digital forms or download PDFs. Scan the QR code here:

---

1. Use the "Insurance Comparison Worksheet" to evaluate which approach might work best for your situation.

2. Contact a long-term care specialist to request personalized policy illustrations based on your age, health, and coverage preferences.

3. Review your health history to identify any potential underwriting concerns.

4. If you're a business owner, explore potential tax advantages for corporate-paid policies.

5. Compare the specific features of policies from multiple carriers to find the best match for your needs and preferences.

CREATING YOUR LONG-TERM CARE PLAN

An effective long-term care plan balances your personal preferences with financial realities and legal protections.

Creating this plan requires understanding your unique risk factors, maximizing available tax advantages, and establishing legal documents that will function properly when care is needed.

This section provides frameworks for personalized risk assessment, tax-efficient funding strategies, and comprehensive legal planning to ensure your wishes are honored even during periods of vulnerability.

ASSESSING YOUR NEEDS

- Generic statistics are less relevant than your unique personal risk factors

- Family health history gives critical insight into potential future care needs

- Current health status and trajectory are predictors of future care needs

- Social support networks impact when and what type of care is needed

- Financial resources determine available care options and sustainability

- Personal preferences should guide care planning decisions

- A structured risk assessment enables targeted, effective planning

BEYOND STATISTICS: YOUR UNIQUE RISK PROFILE

While national statistics provide important context, long-term care planning must be personalized to your specific circumstances.

The often-cited statistic that "70% of people over 65 will need some form of long-term care" offers a general understanding of population-wide risk but tells you little about your individual situation. That number, however, may itself be an underestimate. Alicia H. Munnell, senior advisor at the Center for Retirement Research at Boston College and one of the country's leading voices on retirement security, argues the real figure is closer to 80 percent. In her March 2025 article, "Most Adults Greatly Underestimate the Realities of Aging and Long-Term Care," Munnell makes the case that Americans are systematically unprepared for what lies ahead. Yet even that figure tells you little about your individual situation.

Your personal risk profile is shaped by multiple factors that influence both the likelihood of needing care and the potential duration and cost of that care. Understanding these factors allows you to create a more targeted and effective long-term care plan, one that addresses your specific vulnerabilities rather than generic risks.

BOTTOM LINE: Whether the number is 70% or 80%, national statistics alone aren't as useful for planning as understanding your own personal risk factors. A personalized assessment enables you to create a plan that addresses your specific situation, not average probabilities.

FAMILY HEALTH HISTORY: THE GENETIC BLUEPRINT

Perhaps the most significant predictor of future care needs is your family health history. While not deterministic, genetic factors substantially influence your risk for many conditions that commonly lead to extended care needs.

Longevity patterns in your family deserve particular attention. Exceptional longevity surprisingly increases the likelihood that you'll need care at some point. Those who live into their 90s or beyond have a significantly higher statistical probability of requiring assistance with activities of daily living.[65]

This creates what might seem like a paradox—the longer you live, the more likely you are to need care—but it reflects the reality that extended lifespans often include periods of frailty or impairment.

Specific conditions in your family history warrant careful consideration:

- People with a close relative (such as a parent or sibling) diagnosed with Alzheimer's disease, the most common form of dementia affecting older adults, face an elevated risk. Research on family history suggests this can increase one's relative risk by approximately 30% compared to those without such family history. This represents a proportional increase to whatever your baseline risk might be.[66]

- Family patterns of stroke, particularly early-onset stroke, may indicate genetic predispositions to vascular problems that may lead to both physical and cognitive impairments requiring care.

- Other conditions with genetic components that commonly lead to long-term care needs include Parkinson's disease, cardiovascular disease, and diabetes (having a first-degree relative with Parkinson's increases your risk up to three times).[67]

While having these conditions in your family history doesn't guarantee you'll develop them, they represent important risk factors to consider in your planning.

> **KEY POINT:** Look beyond the superficial family history. Ask not just "Did anyone go to a nursing home?" but "Who needed care of any kind, for how long, and who provided it?" You may discover patterns of care needs that weren't initially obvious.

Creating a comprehensive family health history involves more than simply noting which conditions were present in your family.

For effective extended care planning, document the ages and causes of death for parents, grandparents, and siblings; the age of onset for significant conditions; the duration of care needed for relatives who required assistance; and the care settings utilized by family members.

This information provides valuable insights not just for risk assessment but also for conversations with healthcare providers about preventive measures.

◈ NAVIGATOR STORY

ISAIAH'S FAMILY HISTORY REVELATION

Isaiah, 58, always assumed his care planning needs were minimal. "No one in my family needed nursing home care," he would tell his financial advisor. "We just don't have those problems."

But when his advisor suggested mapping out a more detailed family health history as part of his retirement planning, Isaiah was surprised by what he uncovered.

"While it was true that no one had gone to a nursing home, that wasn't the whole story," Isaiah explains. "My father developed a severe form of neuropathy at age 73 and needed help with daily activities for almost seven years. My mother cared for him at home the entire time, which took a toll on her own health. My grandmother developed vascular dementia after a series of small strokes, and my uncle required ongoing assistance following a heart attack that left him with lasting mobility issues."

This deeper look revealed a family pattern of chronic conditions requiring lengthy care—just not in institutional settings. "I realized care needs were a constant in my family history," Isaiah says. "We simply had a tradition of managing it at home, often at significant cost to the caregivers."

This insight completely changed Isaiah's perspective on long-term care planning. He and his wife implemented a comprehensive plan that included not just financial preparations but also professional care options.

They had open conversations with their children about their wishes, emphasizing their desire to protect their children from the caregiving burden they had witnessed in their own family. Their plan included specific funding for professional care services, ensuring they wouldn't need to rely on their children as primary caregivers.

PERSONAL HEALTH FACTORS: CURRENT STATUS AND TRAJECTORY

Your current health status and health trajectory represent critical components of your risk profile.

Existing chronic conditions and how well they're managed can significantly impact future care needs.

Conditions to pay particular attention to include diabetes, hypertension, heart disease, arthritis, osteoporosis, respiratory conditions, and neurological disorders.[68]

The presence of these conditions doesn't necessarily mean you'll need extended care, but how well they're managed and their progression over time provides important insights into potential future needs.

For example, well-controlled diabetes with no complications presents a different risk profile than poorly controlled diabetes with emerging neuropathy or vision problems.

Your lifestyle factors influence both the likelihood of needing care and your ability to recover from acute health events.

Research consistently shows that lifestyle factors such as the following can significantly impact the onset and progression of conditions that commonly lead to extended care needs.

- Physical activity levels
- Nutritional patterns
- Smoking status
- Alcohol consumption
- Sleep quality
- Stress management
- Social engagement

In addition, regular engagement with preventive healthcare services such as the following can identify issues earlier and potentially delay or reduce care needs.

- Annual physical examinations
- Recommended screenings
- Vaccinations
- Dental and vision care
- Mental health

These all contribute to maintaining health and independence longer. So, your pattern of engagement with these services provides another indicator of potential future needs.

Your current functional status also provides important baseline information for planning. Mobility and balance, strength and endurance, cognitive function, sensory capabilities (vision, hearing), and any existing limitations in activities of daily living offer insights into potential vulnerabilities.

SOCIAL DETERMINANTS: YOUR SUPPORT NETWORK

The strength and proximity of your support network significantly influences both the type of care you may need and when formal care services become necessary. Your family structure affects potential caregiving resources in ways that should be explicitly considered in planning.

Marital status is a significant factor—married individuals typically enter formal care later than single people, as spouses often provide substantial care before outside help becomes necessary. The presence and proximity of adult children, availability of other relatives, and even gender distribution within your family can impact caregiving resources, as daughters are statistically more likely to become caregivers than sons.[69]

Strong social connections correlate with delayed entry into formal care. Friendship circles, community involvement, religious affiliations, and membership in clubs or organizations provide both emotional support and practical assistance that can help maintain independence longer. Research shows that social isolation is a significant risk factor for earlier and more intensive care needs.

Geographic factors influence both care availability and your support network. Proximity to family members, local availability of care services, community resources for aging in place, and even climate considerations that may affect mobility or health conditions all contribute to your care risk profile. Someone living in close proximity to multiple family members in a community with robust senior services has a different risk profile than someone living far from family in an area with limited care resources.

Your living environment affects your ability to remain independent. Home accessibility features, maintenance requirements, proximity to services and healthcare, and community design (walkability, transportation options) all influence how long you can safely remain in your home if impairments develop. For example, a single-level home in a walkable community with nearby services presents fewer challenges than a multi-level home in an isolated area requiring driving for all essential services.

 **NAVIGATOR STORY**

YUMI'S SUPPORT NETWORK

Yumi, a 72-year-old widow who had prudently purchased long-term care insurance in her mid-50's, lives in the same suburban neighborhood where she raised her family. When her financial advisor suggested a long-term care planning review, Yumi confidently stated she had both financial protection and a strong support system.

"I've lived here for 40 years," she explained. "I know everyone, and I have three children who will help if needed."

However, when they mapped out her actual support network, a different picture emerged. Her closest child lived 300 miles away. Her local friends were all approximately her age, facing their own health challenges. Her neighborhood had poor walkability, making it difficult to remain independent if she couldn't drive.

"The exercise was eye-opening," Yumi admits. "I realized that despite having wonderful relationships, my practical day-to-day support system was quite fragile."

This assessment led Yumi to make several proactive changes. She researched senior-friendly housing options in her community, strengthened relationships with younger neighbors, explored transportation alternatives, and discussed realistic expectations with her adult children about the types of support they could provide from a distance.

"I now understand that having a strong social network isn't just about having people who care about you," Yumi says. "It's about having the right supports in the right proximity to help with practical daily needs.

FINANCIAL RESOURCES: THE FOUNDATION OF CHOICE

Your financial resources directly impact the range of care options available to you and your ability to sustain your preferred care setting over time.

> **KEY POINT:** Financial resources don't just determine how much care you can afford—they influence where you receive care, who provides it, and how long you can sustain your preferred arrangements. Financial preparation is about preserving choices, not just paying bills.

A comprehensive assessment of your financial resources provides the foundation for realistic care planning.

Stable, guaranteed income provides a foundation for care planning.

Social Security benefits, pension income, annuity payments, rental income, and required minimum distributions from retirement accounts create a baseline of resources that can help fund ongoing care needs.

The gap between this guaranteed income and potential care costs in your area represents a key planning consideration.

The composition and liquidity of your assets influence care funding strategies.

Retirement accounts, taxable investment accounts, bank accounts and cash equivalents, real estate holdings, business interests, and life insurance cash values all represent potential resources for care funding, but with varying degrees of accessibility, tax implications, and impact on overall financial security.

Outstanding debts can reduce financial flexibility when care needs arise. Mortgage balances, consumer debt, medical debt, and even student loans (increasingly relevant for older adults) may limit your ability to reallocate resources for care needs.

A comprehensive financial assessment should include both assets and liabilities to provide an accurate picture of available resources.

Long-term care insurance, state and federal government programs, and family financial assistance are among the most common supplemental resources to consider in your planning.

Understanding these resources and their limitations is essential for creating a realistic care funding strategy.

PERSONAL PREFERENCES: THE OFTEN-OVERLOOKED FACTOR

Your personal preferences regarding care significantly impact both planning needs and potential costs. These preferences should be explicitly considered and documented as part of your needs assessment.

Where you want to receive care affects your planning strategies. A strong preference for home care (potentially higher cost for 24/7 needs), openness to assisted living, willingness to consider nursing home care if needed, and geographic preferences (remaining in current community versus relocating) all influence the resources required to implement your plan.

Your expectations regarding who provides care shape the

type of plan needed to honor your preferences. This includes your desire to avoid burdening family members, comfort with family caregiving supplemented by professional support, preference for professional caregivers only, and cultural expectations regarding family care. Related to this are your feelings about maintaining control and independence—your willingness to accept care from others, importance of privacy, desire to maintain decision-making authority, and comfort with technology-enabled monitoring or assistance.

Quality expectations regarding care significantly influence cost projections for long-term care. Basic care needs versus premium service expectations, desired staff-to-resident ratios, private accommodations versus shared spaces, and desired amenities and activities all influence the resources required to fund your preferred care approach.

ASSESSING YOUR PERSONAL RISK: A STRUCTURED APPROACH

Most people assess long-term care risk one factor at a time, focusing solely on family history, current health, or financial capacity as if each exists independently. That's a mistake. Your actual risk profile exists at the intersection of multiple factors, and how they interact determines your vulnerability.

A structured assessment identifies both compounding risks (factors that amplify each other) and offsetting strengths (resources that mitigate exposure). This allows you to build a targeted plan rather than react to generic scenarios.

Health Profile: Family History and Current Status

Document your family health history across multiple generations. Create a multi-generational health map identifying patterns of conditions that commonly lead to care needs—Alzheimer's, Parkinson's, stroke, diabetes complications. Note ages of onset and duration of care for affected relatives.

Then assess your current health: existing diagnoses and management, functional capabilities and limitations, recent health trajectory, and specific risks your healthcare providers have flagged.

Assessment tools that help:

- Functional assessments from occupational therapists evaluate current abilities and project how these might change over time

- Home safety evaluations identify factors that increase fall risk or compromise your ability to remain safely at home

- Genetic testing may provide additional risk information for those with strong family histories, though it has limitations and ethical considerations requiring professional guidance

Support Network: Who Shows Up When It Matters

Map your actual support structure. Identify potential family caregivers and their proximity. Assess the reliability of social connections beyond immediate family. Evaluate community resources and local support services. Consider how this network might change over time—adult children relocating, aging friends, shifting family dynamics.

Strong family support can offset financial limitations. Weak or nonexistent support amplifies the need for paid care and professional coordination.

Financial Capacity: Resources and Gaps

Calculate sustainable monthly income from all sources. Assess asset liquidity and accessibility. Compare this against local care costs to identify potential funding gaps. Evaluate whether insurance options align with your financial profile and risk tolerance.

Assessment tools that help:

- Long-term care cost calculators project local care expenses based on current market data
- Financial planning software models the financial impact of various care scenarios

Limited financial resources don't eliminate planning option, they clarify which strategies are viable and which funding gaps require creative solutions.

Personal Preferences: Non-Negotiables and Priorities

Clarify your preferred care settings and arrangements. Specify quality expectations and priorities. Identify the non-negotiable aspects of your future care. Recognize that preferences may shift as needs evolve, but establishing baseline expectations ensures your plan reflects your values, not just financial constraints.

Integration: Where Risk Compounds or Offsets

The real insight comes from analyzing how these factors interact:

- **Compounding risks** – Family history of longevity combined with early cognitive decline signals extended care duration and escalating complexity

- **Offsetting factors** – Limited financial resources but strong, local family support reduces immediate need for paid care and provides coordination capacity

- **Priority assessment** – Focus on risks with both high likelihood and severe impact, not every theoretical possibility

Your unique combination of health, support, finances, and preferences determines which risks require immediate attention and which strategies offer the most protection per dollar invested.

FROM ASSESSMENT TO ACTION: USING YOUR RISK PROFILE

Your personal risk assessment should inform key aspects of your long-term care plan:

Timing and Urgency

Higher-risk profiles suggest more urgent planning needs, particularly for insurance options requiring health qualification. If your assessment reveals compounding risks—family history of early-onset dementia combined with limited financial resources—delaying action reduces your options. While your health is an asset, the door remains open.

Insurance Design Decisions

Your specific risk factors should influence benefit period, monthly benefit amount, and inflation protection. Family history of extended care needs suggests longer benefit periods. Limited family support increases the need for higher monthly benefits to fund professional care. High-cost geographic areas demand stronger inflation protection.

Researching Care Options

If your assessment suggests higher likelihood of needing specific types of care, begin researching options before a crisis occurs. This allows informed decisions about preferred facilities, home care agencies, or continuing care retirement communities while you have time to compare quality, cost, and availability.

Home Modifications and Technology

Identified risk factors may suggest specific modifications to support aging in place. Arthritis or mobility concerns point to bathroom accessibility improvements. Family history of falls suggests grab bars, improved lighting, and removal of trip hazards. Smart home technology can compensate for potential physical limitations.

Incapacity Planning

Risk factors such as family history of dementia highlight the importance of comprehensive incapacity planning through advance directives and powers of attorney, with specific provisions addressing vulnerabilities identified in your assessment.

Family Conversations

Your risk assessment provides a factual foundation for conversations about potential future care needs and responsibilities. Rather than discussing hypothetical scenarios, focus on specific vulnerabilities and develop targeted strategies to address them. This shifts the conversation from abstract worry to concrete planning.

BOTTOM LINE: This assessment isn't about predicting your future with certainty. It's about identifying your specific vulnerabilities so you can build a targeted plan that addresses real risks, not generic fears. Your unique combination of health, support, finances, and preferences determines which risks demand immediate attention and which strategies deliver the most protection.

THE LARSENS' TARGETED PLANNING

Stefan and Anika Larsen, both 62, approached long-term care planning systematically rather than reactively. After completing a comprehensive needs assessment with their financial advisor, they identified their specific risk factors and strengths.

Their assessment revealed that Stefan had a family history of cardio-vascular disease with subsequent physical limitations, while Anika's family showed patterns of longevity with cognitive decline. Their financial resources were solid but not unlimited, and they had three adult children scattered across the country.

"The assessment helped us create a very targeted plan," Anika explains. "Instead of generic planning, we focused on our specific vulnerabilities."

Their resulting plan included several customized elements:

- *A long-term care insurance policy with a longer benefit period for Anika than Stefan, reflecting their different risk profiles*
- *Smart home technology to compensate for potential physical limitations*
- *A phased home modification plan prioritizing bathroom accessibility*
- *Comprehensive powers of attorney with specific provisions for cognitive decline*
- *Regular cognitive assessments as part of their annual physicals*

"Without the structured assessment, we might have created a generic plan that missed our specific needs," says Stefan. "Now we feel our plan addresses our actual risks, not just statistical possibilities."

☑ ACTION STEPS CHECKLIST

All worksheets and templates for this book are online at
WWW.YOURRETIREMENTBLINDSPOT.COM/RESOURCES
Complete them as digital forms or download PDFs. Scan the QR code here:

1. Create a detailed family health history map going back at least two generations.

2. Schedule a wellness assessment with your primary care provider, focused specifically on functional abilities and limitations.

3. Map your current support network, identifying who could realistically provide various types of assistance if needed.

4. Document your care preferences, including setting, caregiver type, and quality expectations.

5. Complete a comprehensive risk assessment that integrates health, social, financial, and preference factors.

TAX ADVANTAGE PLANNING

CHAPTER AT A GLANCE

- *Strategic tax planning can reduce the cost of long-term care coverage*

- *Tax-qualified long-term care insurance premiums (defined under IRC Section 7702B) may be tax-deductible, subject to age-based limits*

- *Beginning in 2026, distributions from certain employer retirement plans to pay tax-qualified long-term care insurance premiums avoid the 10% early withdrawal penalty for individuals under age 59½*

- *Health Savings Accounts (HSAs) may offer a triple tax advantage and can be used, in some cases, to pay qualified long-term care insurance premiums up to IRS limits*

- *The Pension Protection Act created powerful tax benefits for certain asset-based products*

- *Business owners have extra tax advantages for long-term care coverage*

- *Integrating long-term care planning with tax and estate strategies can help reduce taxes and preserve your legacy*

- *Tax laws are complex and change frequently, requiring expert guidance*

THE TAX DIMENSION OF LONG-TERM CARE PLANNING

The Health Insurance Portability and Accountability Act (HIPAA) of 1996 created tax advantages for long-term care insurance policies that meet federal standards under Internal Revenue Code (IRC) Section 7702B.[70]

These tax advantages apply to both traditional tax-qualified long-term care insurance and the long-term care components of tax-qualified hybrid products.

To qualify for these tax benefits, a policy must meet specific requirements under IRC Section 7702B:

- **Focus on qualified long-term care services.** Coverage is limited to services for individuals with a certified chronic illness, such as those unable to perform at least two daily activities (e.g., bathing, dressing, eating, toileting, transferring, or continence) for at least 90 days or those with severe cognitive impairments, like Alzheimer's, requiring significant supervision.

- **Guaranteed renewal.** The policy must be renewable as long as premiums are paid, protecting policyholders from cancellation due to age or declining health.

- **No cash value for long-term care benefits.** The long-term care portion of the policy cannot offer a cash surrender value. In hybrid products, any cash value belongs to the life insurance or annuity component, keeping long-term care benefits dedicated to care expenses.

- **Smart use of refunds and dividends.** Any premium refunds or dividends must reduce future premiums or enhance future benefits, ensuring the policy prioritizes long-term care support.

- **Adherence to consumer protections.** The policy must follow standards set by the National Association of Insurance Commissioners (NAIC), including clear disclosures and safeguards against unfair marketing.

- **No overlap with Medicare.** Coverage cannot include expenses already paid by Medicare, except when Medicare is a secondary payer.

By meeting these standards, qualified long-term care insurance policies offer valuable tax benefits while ensuring coverage is tailored to essential care needs.

Premium Deductibility

One of the key tax advantages of tax-qualified long-term care insurance (as defined under Internal Revenue Code Section 7702B) is the ability to deduct premiums as medical expenses, provided you itemize deductions on Schedule A (Form 1040), subject to specific limitations.

Premiums for tax-qualified long-term care insurance may be deductible as medical expenses, subject to two important limitations:

First, medical expenses, including long-term care insurance premiums, must exceed 7.5% of adjusted gross income to be deductible when itemizing.[71] This high threshold is difficult for many people to reach in practice. Since fewer taxpayers itemize deductions today, and this percentage requirement demands substantial medical expenses, many policyholders don't actually benefit from this deduction despite its availability.

Second, the IRS establishes maximum deductible amounts based on the taxpayer's age at the end of the tax year.

For 2026, these limits are:[72]

- Age 40 or under: $500
- Age 41-50: $930
- Age 51-60: $1,860
- Age 61-70: $4,960
- Age 71 and older: $6,200

These limits are adjusted annually for inflation and apply per person, not per policy. For a married couple, each spouse can deduct up to the age-based limit that applies to them individually when itemizing deductions.

2026 Game-Changer: Tapping Retirement Accounts Without the Penalty

Here's a problem you've probably thought about: Long-term care insurance makes the most sense to purchase in your 40s and

50s—your health window is open, premiums are lower, and you have leverage. But if you have money sitting in a 401(k) or 403(b) and try to access it before age 59½, you get hit with a 10% early withdrawal penalty on top of ordinary income taxes.

It's been a frustrating catch-22: use retirement savings to protect retirement savings, but pay a penalty for doing so.

That changes in 2026.

Section 334 of the SECURE 2.0 Act eliminates the 10% early withdrawal penalty when you use funds from certain employer-sponsored retirement plans specifically to pay premiums for tax-qualified long-term care insurance under IRC Section 7702B.[73]

What you need to know:

The withdrawal is still taxed as ordinary income. The new rule only waives the additional 10% penalty that typically applies to early distributions under IRC §72(t).

This applies to 401(k), 403(b), 403(a), and governmental 457(b) plans, but there's a catch: your employer must amend the plan to allow it. Plan sponsors aren't required to offer this feature, so you'll need to check with your plan administrator.

Whether traditional IRAs qualify is still uncertain. Until the IRS issues final guidance, assume only employer-sponsored plans are eligible.

How much can you withdraw?

Your annual withdrawal is capped at the smallest of three amounts:

- The actual premiums you paid for qualified coverage that year

- 10% of your vested account balance in that plan

- $2,600 for 2026 (indexed annually for inflation)

For many individuals and couples in their planning years, $2,600 can cover a substantial portion of annual premiums, depending on age, health, and the coverage you choose.

Why this matters:

This provision removes a real barrier. If you've been delaying coverage because you didn't want to pay current premiums out of pocket, or worse, face a penalty to access your own retirement money, you now have a more efficient path forward.

Your health window won't stay open forever. This rule gives you one more tool to act while you still have leverage.

> **BOTTOM LINE:** The 2026 rule removes a real barrier by waiving the 10% early withdrawal penalty when using retirement funds to pay for tax-qualified long-term care insurance premiums. The distribution remains taxable as ordinary income, but eliminating the penalty makes this funding strategy far more efficient. Check with your plan administrator and tax professional before proceeding.

Tax-Free Benefits

Another significant tax advantage of qualified long-term care insurance is that benefits are generally received tax-free, though specific rules apply. Benefits from qualified long-term care insurance policies are typically excluded from taxable income, with the following limitations:[74]

- For policies that reimburse actual expenses, all benefits are received tax-free.

- For fixed-amount policies that pay a set daily amount regardless of expenses incurred, benefits are tax-free up to the greater of actual qualified long-term care expenses or the HIPAA per diem limit ($430 per day for 2026, adjusted annually for inflation).[75]

- Any benefits received above these limits may be taxable as ordinary income.

Consult with a tax professional regarding your specific situation.

> **BOTTOM LINE:** The tax benefits of tax-qualified long-term care insurance (IRC Section 7702B) can reduce the effective cost of coverage for some taxpayers, but these benefits are often underutilized. While tax advantages shouldn't be the primary driver of your long-term care planning decisions, they represent an important factor that should be incorporated into your overall strategy.

HSA STRATEGIES FOR LONG-TERM CARE PLANNING

Health Savings Accounts (HSAs) offer unique advantages for long-term care planning, combining immediate tax deductions, tax-free growth, and tax-free withdrawals for qualified expenses.

This "triple tax advantage," including an above-the-line deduction for contributions, which reduces your taxable income even if you don't itemize, makes HSAs one of the most tax-efficient funding vehicles available for extended care planning.

To contribute to an HSA, you must be covered by a high-deductible health plan (HDHP), not be enrolled in Medicare, and not be claimed as a dependent on someone else's tax return. For 2026, contribution limits are $4,400 for individual coverage and $8,750 for family coverage, with an additional $1,000 catch-up contributions allowed for those 55 and older.[76]

HSA funds can be used tax-free to pay tax-qualified long-term care insurance premiums, subject to the same age-based limits that apply to medical expense deductions. This provides a way to effectively pay premiums with pretax dollars, even if you don't itemize deductions or have enough medical expenses to exceed the 7.5% AGI threshold.[77]

> **KEY POINT:** HSAs offer a "triple tax advantage": above-the-line contributions, tax-free growth, and tax-free withdrawals for tax-qualified long-term care premiums (up to IRS limits). This makes them one of the most tax-efficient ways to fund long-term care.

Several strategic considerations can enhance the value of HSAs for extended care planning.

Consider maximizing HSA contributions during your working years, using other funds for current medical expenses, and allowing the HSA to grow for future long-term care needs. This approach leverages the tax-free growth potential of the HSA over time.

If one spouse owns an HSA, they can use those funds to pay qualified long-term care insurance premiums for themselves, their spouse, and any tax dependents, even if only one spouse is covered by a high-deductible health plan. This creates planning opportunities for couples where only one spouse has HSA eligibility.[78]

Once enrolled in Medicare, you can no longer contribute to an HSA, but you can continue to use existing HSA funds for long-term care premiums and expenses.

From a legacy planning perspective, HSAs can be left to a spouse with continued tax advantages, though non-spouse beneficiaries will generally need to include the HSA value in taxable income. This makes HSAs more valuable for funding care during life than as legacy assets.[79]

 **NAVIGATOR STORY**

OLLIE & JUSTIN'S TAX SURPRISE

Justin and Ollie, both 51, met with their advisor Lisa to discuss long-term care planning. They had already purchased comprehensive long-term care policies with annual premiums of $5,600 combined.

"We're committed to protection, but looking for tax-efficient ways to pay the premiums," Justin explained.

Lisa noted they both had access to Health Savings Accounts through their employers' High-Deductible Health Plans. "Your HSAs can pay a portion of those premiums with pre-tax dollars," she explained. "For 2025, the IRS allows each of you to use up to $1,800 from your HSAs for long-term care premiums based on your age bracket."

The couple implemented her advice: they maximized their HSA contributions and used $3,600 annually ($1,800 each) to pay a big portion of their long-term care insurance premiums, staying within the 2025 IRS age-based limits.

"Unlike medical expense deductions that require itemizing and exceeding 7.5% of your AGI, HSA contributions reduce your taxable income regardless,"Lisa explained. "It's an above-the-line deduction."

"We're essentially paying a large portion of our premiums with pre-tax dollars," Ollie noted. "And since we're contributing the maximum to our HSAs, we still have additional funds for other qualified medical expenses."

Their HSA strategy created a tax-efficient approach to funding their existing long-term care protection.

This hypothetical scenario is for illustrative purposes only. Actual tax benefits depend on individual circumstances and current tax law. Consult a qualified tax advisor for details.

THE PENSION PROTECTION ACT: TRANSFORMING ANNUITIES AND LIFE INSURANCE

The Pension Protection Act of 2006 created significant tax advantages for certain asset-based long-term care products, particularly when funded through 1035 exchanges from existing life insurance or non-qualified annuity contracts. This legislation has transformed the long-term care planning landscape by enabling new tax-efficient funding options.

The Act allows tax-free 1035 exchanges from existing life insurance policies or non-qualified annuity contracts into qualified long-term care insurance or combination products.[80]

This enables policyholders to reposition assets that might otherwise generate taxable income into products that provide tax-free long-term care benefits.

Perhaps most significantly, long-term care benefits received from qualifying combination products are generally income tax-free, even when paid from the gain portion of a non-qualified annuity contract.[81][82] his represents a powerful planning opportunity, particularly for non-qualified annuities with substantial built-in gains that would otherwise be taxed as ordinary income upon withdrawal.

In some cases, partial exchanges can be executed, allowing for strategic repositioning of a portion of an existing contract's value. This provides flexibility for those who wish to maintain some of their original coverage while adding long-term care protection.

This provision creates several strategic applications for extended care planning.

For instance, older life insurance or non-qualified deferred annuity contracts with substantial gains can be exchanged into hybrid or combination long-term care products, potentially transforming taxable gains into tax-free benefits for qualifying care.

Another key strategy involves "rescuing" older life insurance policies at risk of lapsing or requiring premium increases by exchanging them into paid-up combination products, which preserves both death benefits and adds long-term care protection.

These approaches turn potential financial vulnerabilities into proactive safeguards, offering individuals the opportunity to maintain control over their legacy without unnecessary tax burdens.

 **NAVIGATOR STORY**

SALVADOR'S ANNUITY TRANSFORMATION

Salvador, 70, had purchased a non-qualified deferred annuity 15 years earlier with a $100,000 premium. The annuity had grown to $215,000, meaning he had $115,000 in taxable gain that would be subject to ordinary income tax rates upon withdrawal.

"I was essentially stuck," Salvador explains. "I didn't need the income, but I was concerned about future long-term care costs. If I surrendered the annuity to pay for care, I'd face a significant tax bill on the gains."

After consulting with his financial advisor, Salvador executed a tax-free 1035 exchange of his deferred annuity into a combination annuity/long-term care product under the Pension Protection Act provisions.

"The exchange accomplished multiple objectives," he says. "I pre-served my principal, locked in a new death benefit, gained substantial long-term care protection, and—most importantly—ensured that all benefits, including those paid from the gain portion, would be received tax-free if I needed care."

This strategy effectively transformed what would have been taxable income into tax-free long-term care benefits, significantly enhancing the efficiency of Salvador's long-term care planning.

BUSINESS OWNER ADVANTAGES: ENHANCED TAX BENEFITS

Business owners can leverage tax strategies for long-term care insurance, varying by business structure, offering efficiencies unavailable to non-business owners. This allows for smarter financial planning, reducing costs while providing essential protection for owners and employees alike.[83]

C-Corporations provide the most favorable treatment: premiums for tax-qualified LTCI (long-term care insurance) paid for employees, including owner-employees, are fully deductible without age-based limits, excluded from the employee's taxable income, and benefits are tax-free.[84]

Unlike health insurance, LTCI can be offered selectively to key employees or owners through executive carve-out plans, without the need to cover all employees equally. This flexibility helps businesses reward top talent or protect family members involved in the company.[85]

For pass-through entities like S-Corporations, partnerships, and LLCs, tax treatment depends on ownership. Premiums for >2% owners are included in their income but can be deducted as self-employed health insurance, subject to 2026 age-based limits ($500 for 40 or under, $930 for 41-50, $1,860 for 51-60, $4,960 for 61-70, $6,200 for 71 and older), on their personal tax return. This "above-the-line" deduction is available even if they don't itemize deductions, a benefit also available to sole proprietors.[86]

For <2% owners and regular employees, premiums are excluded from income, and benefits are received tax-free.[87] Sole proprietors can deduct premiums similarly as self-employed health insurance, bypassing the 7.5% AGI threshold that often limits individual deductions.[88]

For key employees or when direct premium payment isn't ideal, a Section 162 bonus plan offers flexibility: the business provides taxable compensation specifically for purchasing LTCI, deducts it as a business expense, and the employee may deduct the premiums as a medical expense, subject to itemization rules and limitations.[89] [90]

> **BOTTOM LINE:** Business owners have unique tax advantages for long-term care planning that are often overlooked. These strategies can reduce the after-tax cost of coverage while providing valuable benefits to key people in the business. Proper structuring is essential to maximize tax efficiency while maintaining compliance with relevant regulations.

HYBRID LONG-TERM CARE: TAX CONSIDERATIONS AND PLANNING INTEGRATION

Asset-based or hybrid long-term care products combine life insurance or annuity benefits with long-term care protection, offering unique tax advantages that should be integrated with your broader financial planning.

> **KEY POINT:** Tax planning for long-term care should be viewed as a dynamic, ongoing process. Regularly review your strategy as tax laws, your health status, and your financial situation evolve over time.

Key Tax Features:

- For life insurance/LTC combinations, only the portion attributable to the tax-qualified long-term care component may be deductible as a medical expense.

- Life insurance death benefits are generally received income tax-free by beneficiaries if long-term care benefits aren't fully utilized.

- Under the Pension Protection Act, qualifying combination annuities allow for tax-free long-term care benefits, even when paid from the gain portion of the contract.

- Existing annuities with substantial gains can be exchanged into combination products, potentially converting taxable gains into tax-free long-term care benefits.

Strategic Planning Opportunities:

- IRA Qualified Charitable Distributions (for those 70½ or older) can reduce adjusted gross income, potentially enhancing the deductibility of long-term care premiums.

- Strategic Roth conversions during lower-income years can help manage future taxable income.

- Hybrid long-term care products owned by a properly structured Irrevocable Life Insurance Trust (ILIT) can provide care benefits during life while keeping death benefits outside the taxable estate.

- "Deduction bunching" by timing discretionary medical expenses and premium payments in specific years can help exceed the 7.5% AGI threshold for deductibility.

WORKING WITH TAX PROFESSIONALS

The tax aspects of long-term care planning are complex and frequently changing. Working with knowledgeable tax professionals is essential for maximizing available benefits while ensuring compliance with tax laws.

When selecting tax advisors for long-term care planning, look for:

- Experience with long-term care insurance taxation
- Familiarity with business entity taxation if applicable
- Understanding of the intersection between tax planning and Medicaid eligibility
- Ability to coordinate with your financial advisor and insurance professional

Regular review of your long-term care tax strategy is important, as both tax laws and personal circumstances change over time. Consider scheduling annual reviews that specifically address the tax efficiency of your extended care plan.

By incorporating tax planning into your long-term care strategy, you can potentially reduce costs, increase available benefits, and enhance the overall efficiency of your plan.

As stated previously, tax advantages should never be the primary driver of extended care planning decisions, they represent an important dimension that should not be overlooked.

All worksheets and templates for this book are online at
WWW.YOURRETIREMENTBLINDSPOT.COM/RESOURCES
Complete them as digital forms or download PDFs. Scan the QR code here: 

---

1. Review your current medical expenses to determine if you meet the 7.5% AGI threshold for deducting long-term care insurance premiums.

2. If you have HSA eligibility, calculate the maximum allowable contribution and consider earmarking a portion for future long-term care needs.

3. Inventory existing life insurance policies and annuity contracts to identify potential 1035 exchange opportunities.

4. Business owners should schedule a consultation with tax and financial advisors to explore business-specific tax advantages.

5. Create a multi-year tax strategy that coordinates long-term care planning with broader tax considerations such as retirement account distributions and capital gains management.

LEGAL CONSIDERATIONS

- Proper legal documents ensure your wishes are followed even if you can't communicate

- Powers of Attorney for finances and healthcare are essential for avoiding guardianship

- Advance directives provide specific instructions for medical treatment preferences

- Trusts can protect assets while ensuring proper use of funds for care

- Specialized care coordination documents address quality-of-life preferences

- Regular review and updating of legal documents is critical as circumstances change

- Professional guidance helps navigate complex legal requirements

BEYOND FUNDING: THE LEGAL FRAMEWORK FOR LONG-TERM CARE

While financial planning for long-term care is essential, equally important is establishing the legal framework that ensures your wishes are honored and your interests protected if you become unable to manage your own affairs.

Without proper legal planning, even the most robust financial strategy may fail to achieve your goals when care is needed.

The legal aspects of long-term care planning extend far beyond basic estate planning documents.

They include specialized provisions to address care preferences, decision-making authority during periods of incapacity, and mechanisms to ensure resources are used appropriately for your benefit.

This chapter explores the key legal components of a comprehensive extended care plan and how they work together to protect you and your loved ones.

POWERS OF ATTORNEY: EXTENDING YOUR VOICE

A power of attorney (POA) is a legal document that authorizes someone (your "agent" or "attorney-in-fact") to act on your behalf.

State laws vary regarding POA requirements and recognition. Some financial institutions may require their own POA forms or may not honor older documents. It's important to review and update your POA regularly and consult an attorney familiar with your state's laws.

In the context of extended care planning, two types of powers of attorney are particularly important:

- Financial
- Healthcare

Note: In some states, a healthcare power of attorney may be called a "healthcare proxy" or "medical power of attorney."

Durable Financial Power of Attorney

This document authorizes your agent to manage your financial affairs if you become incapacitated.

Without this document, your family might need to pursue guardianship or conservatorship through the courts—a process that can be time-consuming, expensive, and public.

When creating a financial power of attorney for long-term care planning, several key considerations should be addressed.

The scope of authority granted to your agent is perhaps the most important decision. You can grant broad powers or limit your agent's authority to specific transactions or accounts.

For long-term care planning, consider whether your agent will need authority to pay for care services and related expenses, access financial accounts and safe deposit boxes, manage real estate (including possible sale of your home), handle insurance matters (including filing claims), manage investments and retirement accounts, apply for government benefits (including Medicaid), and continue your pattern of financial support for dependents or charities.

The effective date of the power is another important consideration. A "springing" power of attorney becomes effective only when you're declared incapacitated, while an "immediate" power of attorney takes effect upon signing.

For long-term care planning, immediate powers often provide more seamless transitions but require absolute trust in your agent.

Naming successor agents ensures continuity if your primary agent becomes unavailable or unable to serve.

Consider including explicit requirements for your agent to maintain records and provide periodic accountings to family members or advisors.

If your long-term care plan includes potential Medicaid planning, specific gifting powers may be necessary but should be carefully limited and defined.[91]

Improperly drafted gifting powers can result in Medicaid penalties or disqualification. Always consult an elder law attorney for guidance on Medicaid planning.

Healthcare Power of Attorney

This document (sometimes called a healthcare proxy) authorizes your agent to make medical decisions on your behalf if you cannot communicate your wishes.

This is particularly crucial for extended care situations, where ongoing healthcare decisions may be required.

When selecting a healthcare agent, look for someone who understands your values and preferences, is willing to advocate for you, and is able to make difficult decisions under pressure.

While not absolutely necessary, having an agent who lives near you can be advantageous for urgent decisions and ongoing oversight of care.

Ensure your document complies with HIPAA (Health Insurance Portability and Accountability Act) requirements, allowing your agent to access your medical records and speak with healthcare providers.

Consider whether your agent should have authority to:

- Select and change healthcare providers

- Approve or decline specific treatments

- Access medical records

- Authorize admission to or discharge from healthcare facilities

- Implement or continue your advance directives

- Make decisions about participation in research studies

While advance directives (discussed below) typically address end-of-life care, your healthcare POA can include guidance about extended care preferences, such as home care versus facility care when feasible.

BOTTOM LINE: Generic powers of attorney rarely address the specific needs of long-term care situations. A properly drafted financial power of attorney should include explicit authority to implement your long-term care plan, including managing insurance policies, paying care providers, and accessing resources earmarked for care. Similarly, healthcare powers of attorney should address not just end-of-life decisions but ongoing care preferences and quality-of-life considerations.

 **NAVIGATOR STORY**

JAVIER & LORENA

When Javier began showing signs of cognitive decline at age 72, his wife Lorena assumed she could handle their financial affairs since they owned most assets jointly. However, when she needed to access Javier's retirement account to pay for his increasing care needs, she discovered she had no legal authority to do so.

"I thought being his wife gave me automatic rights," Lorena explains. "I was shocked to learn I needed to petition the court for guardianship, a process that took months and cost thousands in legal fees."

The guardianship process required Lorena to publicly document Javier's cognitive decline, submit to court oversight, and provide ongoing financial reports. "It was invasive and stressful during an already difficult time," she says. "If we'd had proper powers of attorney in place, we could have avoided all of that."

Javier and Lorena's experience is unfortunately common. Many couples assume that joint ownership of assets or marital status provides sufficient legal authority to manage affairs if one becomes incapacitated. Without comprehensive powers of attorney, however, family members often face unnecessary legal complications precisely when they need to focus on care.

Note: Laws regarding guardianship, powers of attorney, and spousal rights vary by state. Consult with an elder law attorney in your state to understand the specific requirements and protections in your jurisdiction.

ADVANCE DIRECTIVES: ENSURING YOUR WISHES ARE HONORED

Advance directives are legal documents that specify your preferences for medical treatment if you become unable to communicate.

While often associated with end-of-life care, these documents also have important implications for extended care situations.

Living Will

A living will specifies your preferences regarding life-sustaining treatments in terminal conditions or permanent unconsciousness.

While primarily focused on end-of-life care, a living will can influence extended care by clarifying your values regarding quality of life versus longevity.

When creating a living will, consider the balance between specificity and flexibility.

Overly specific directives may not address unforeseen circumstances, while overly general statements may provide insufficient guidance. Consider balancing clear statements of your values with reasonable flexibility for your healthcare agent.

Medical technologies and your own preferences may change over time.

Regular review and updating of your living will ensures it continues to reflect your wishes.

Ensure your living will is readily accessible to your healthcare agent, family members, and healthcare providers. Consider registering it with your state's advance directive registry if available.

POLST/MOLST Forms

Physician Orders for Life-Sustaining Treatment (POLST) or Medical Orders for Life-Sustaining Treatment (MOLST) forms translate your advance directives into specific medical orders that emergency personnel and healthcare providers must follow.

These forms are particularly relevant for individuals already in extended care situations or with advanced illness.

Unlike advance directives, which you can complete independently, POLST/MOLST forms require physician participation and signature.

These forms are designed to follow you across care settings, ensuring consistency in treatment approaches.

As your condition changes, your POLST/MOLST form should be reviewed and potentially revised to reflect current circumstances and preferences.[92]

> **KEY POINT:** Standard advance directives primarily address end-of-life care but may not provide sufficient guidance for long-term care decisions. Consider supplementing these documents with a detailed statement of care preferences addressing where and how you wish to receive care if you develop chronic care needs.

GUARDIANSHIP AND CONSERVATORSHIP: THE COURT ALTERNATIVE

If you become incapacitated without having executed powers of attorney, the court may appoint a guardian (for personal decisions) or conservator (for financial decisions) to manage your affairs.

Understanding this process is important, as it represents the default legal mechanism in the absence of proper planning.

Court-appointed guardians or conservators may not know your preferences or values, potentially leading to decisions you would not have chosen.

Guardianship proceedings are public, potentially exposing private financial and personal information. Legal fees, court costs, and ongoing reporting requirements can significantly reduce assets available for your care.

In the absence of clear documentation of your wishes, family members may disagree about appropriate care decisions, potentially leading to contentious legal proceedings.

Court-appointed guardians are typically limited to the jurisdiction of the appointing court, creating complications for individuals who own property in multiple states or who relocate for care.[93]

The guardianship process varies by state but generally involves a court petition, medical certification of incapacity, notice to interested parties, a hearing, and ongoing court supervision.

This process can be emotionally difficult, expensive, and time-consuming—precisely when families are already dealing with the stress of a loved one's incapacity.

Proper advance planning with comprehensive powers of attorney and other legal documents can help avoid this outcome in most cases.

TRUSTS: PROTECTING ASSETS AND DIRECTING CARE

Trusts can serve multiple purposes in extended care planning, from asset protection to ensuring funds are used appropriately for your care.

Different types of trusts offer various benefits and limitations that should be carefully considered based on your specific circumstances.

Revocable Living Trusts

While primarily used for probate avoidance, revocable living trusts can include provisions for management of your assets if you become incapacitated. This creates a seamless transition of control without court involvement.

Assets must be properly titled in the name of the trust to avoid probate and enable incapacity management. Your successor trustee will manage trust assets for your benefit if you become incapacitated, making this selection as important as your power of attorney agent.

The trust can include specific instructions regarding your care preferences and how assets should be used to support those preferences. Your revocable trust and powers of attorney should work together seamlessly, with clear delineation of which document takes precedence for specific decisions.[94]

Irrevocable Trusts

In some cases, irrevocable trusts may be used as part of extended care planning, particularly when asset protection or Medicaid planning is a consideration. Once assets are placed in an irrevocable trust, you generally cannot change the terms or directly access the principal.

Transfers to irrevocable trusts are typically subject to Medicaid's five-year look-back period and may affect eligibility. Irrevocable trusts have distinct income, gift, and estate tax implications that should be carefully evaluated.[95]

The trustee's authority to use trust assets for your care should be clearly defined, particularly regarding discretionary distributions.

Special Needs Trusts

For individuals with disabilities, special needs trusts can provide for supplemental care needs while preserving eligibility for government benefits.

First-party trusts (funded with the beneficiary's own assets) require Medicaid payback provisions, while third-party trusts (funded by others) do not.

The trustee must understand both the beneficiary's needs and the complex rules governing benefit eligibility. The trust should clearly define what expenses can be paid to supplement rather than replace government benefits.[96]

CARE COORDINATION DOCUMENTS: BEYOND TRADITIONAL LEGAL PLANNING

Beyond standard legal documents, several specialized documents can enhance your extended care plan by providing detailed guidance to your representatives and caregivers.

Personal Care Plan

This non-binding but valuable document outlines your preferences regarding daily routines, personal care, living environment, social activities, and other quality-of-life considerations.

Key elements include:

- Daily routine preferences (preferred wake/sleep times, meal preferences, bathing preferences, and other daily habits)

- Environmental preferences (temperature, lighting, noise levels, and other comfort factors)

- Social engagement (desired frequency and types of social interaction)

- Spiritual practices (religious services, meditation, or other spiritual activities important to you)

- Recreational activities (hobbies, interests, and activities you wish to continue)

- Dietary preferences (food preferences, restrictions, and mealtime routines)

- Personal appearance (clothing preferences, grooming standards, and other aspects of personal presentation)
- Caregiver Instructions

This document provides specific guidance to family caregivers or professional care providers about your care needs and preferences. Key elements include:

- Medical conditions (summary of conditions requiring monitoring or management)
- Medication schedule (list of medications with dosages, timing, and special instructions)
- Warning signs (symptoms that should prompt medical attention)
- Mobility assistance (specific techniques for transfers or ambulation assistance)
- Communication strategies (effective approaches if communication becomes difficult)
- Behavioral considerations (triggers for distress and effective calming techniques)
- Emergency contacts (prioritized list of who to contact in various situations)

Family Communication Plan

This document outlines how and when family members should be informed about changes in your condition or care needs, helping to prevent misunderstandings and conflicts. Key elements include:

- Communication hierarchy (who should be informed first about various types of changes)

- Communication methods (preferred methods for different situations)

- Decision-making process (how family members should collaborate on major decisions)

- Conflict resolution (process for addressing disagreements about care decisions)

- Visiting guidelines (expectations regarding family visits and involvement)

 NAVIGATOR STORY

THE GARCIA FAMILY

When Maria Garcia was diagnosed with Alzheimer's disease, her children—four siblings living in different states—initially struggled to coordinate her care. "We were constantly miscommunicating," explains her daughter Elena. "Someone would make a decision about Mom's care without telling everyone else, leading to confusion and sometimes arguments."

The situation improved dramatically when the family worked with an elder law attorney to create not just traditional legal documents, but also a detailed family communication plan."

We established clear protocols for who would be notified about what, and in what order," says Elena. "We created a Google document titled "Mom Care Journal" where whoever visited Mom would post updates, and we scheduled monthly video calls to discuss her care. For major decisions, we agreed unanimously on a process that gave everyone input while respecting Mom's wishes."

The communication plan helped the siblings navigate several difficult transitions in their mother's care, from hiring home care to eventually moving Maria to assisted living. "Having a structured way to communicate about Mom's care preserved both her dignity and our relationships with each other," Elena says.

LEGAL PLANNING FOR COUPLES: SPECIAL CONSIDERATIONS

Couples face unique legal planning challenges, particularly when one spouse requires extended care while the other remains independent.

Each spouse should have their own powers of attorney, with potentially different agents for each.

Legal strategies may be needed to protect assets for the healthy spouse while ensuring the ill spouse qualifies for benefits if appropriate.

Understanding Medicaid spousal impoverishment protections is essential for couples considering Medicaid for nursing home care.

Planning should address potential estate recovery claims against the couple's home or other assets after both spouses have passed away.

Retirement account beneficiary designations should be coordinated with the overall extended care plan, particularly when qualified retirement assets represent a significant portion of the couple's wealth.[97]

> **BOTTOM LINE:** Comprehensive long-term care planning requires both financial and legal components working in harmony. Without proper legal documents, even the best financial plan may fail at the critical moment when care is needed. Similarly, legal documents alone cannot create the resources needed to fund quality care. The most effective approach integrates both dimensions to create a cohesive strategy that addresses all aspects of long-term care needs.

KEEPING LEGAL DOCUMENTS CURRENT AND ACCESSIBLE

Even the most carefully crafted legal documents are of limited value if they're outdated or inaccessible when needed.

Regular review triggers include life changes (marriage, divorce, death of named agents, relocation to another state), health changes (new diagnoses that may affect care needs or decision-making capacity), financial changes (significant changes in asset composition or value), legal changes (updates to relevant state or federal laws), and relationship changes (changes in relationships with named agents or family members).

Several accessibility strategies can ensure your documents are available when needed. Ensure all named agents know they've been selected and have copies of relevant documents.

Maintain a secure but accessible location for original documents, with information provided to key individuals about how to access them.

Consider secure digital storage with appropriate access provisions for authorized individuals.

Ensure your primary healthcare providers have current copies of your healthcare directives and power of attorney.

Consider carrying a card in your wallet indicating the existence and location of your advance directives and the contact information for your healthcare agent.

WORKING WITH ELDER LAW ATTORNEYS

The legal aspects of extended care planning are complex and state-specific.

Working with an attorney who specializes in elder law or estate planning with an emphasis on long-term care issues is highly recommended.

When selecting an attorney, look for those who focus specifically on elder law, estate planning, or special needs planning.

Consider attorneys certified in Elder Law by the National Elder Law Foundation or who are members of the National Academy of Elder Law Attorneys (NAELA).

The best elder law attorneys work collaboratively with financial advisors, care managers, and healthcare providers to create comprehensive plans.

Choose an attorney who explains complex concepts clearly and respects your values and preferences.

> **KEY POINT:** Legal documents aren't "set it and forget it" instruments. They should be reviewed regularly—at least every 3-5 years, or when significant life changes occur. Documents created in one state may not work optimally if you relocate to another state.

Typical services provided by elder law attorneys include:

- Document preparation (creating or updating powers of attorney, advance directives, and trusts)

- Medicaid planning (strategies to protect assets while qualifying for benefits if appropriate)

- Veterans benefits (assistance with applications for VA Aid and Attendance benefits)

- Guardianship alternatives (exploring less restrictive alternatives to court-appointed guardianship)

- Care advocacy (assistance with healthcare decision-making and care transitions)

- Family mediation (resolving conflicts among family members regarding care decisions)

THE INTERSECTION OF LEGAL AND FINANCIAL PLANNING

Legal and financial planning for extended care should be coordinated to ensure consistency and effectiveness.

Key coordination points include:

- Asset titling (ensuring asset ownership aligns with your legal documents, particularly trusts)

- Beneficiary designations (coordinating beneficiary designations on insurance policies, retirement accounts, and other assets with your overall plan)

- Insurance integration (ensuring your legal documents authorize your agents to manage insurance policies, file claims, and interact with insurance companies)

- Tax planning (coordinating legal strategies with tax planning to minimize tax impact on care funding)

- Spending authority (ensuring your financial power of attorney explicitly authorizes your agent to implement your extended care funding strategy or liquidating assets if necessary)

By establishing a comprehensive legal framework for your extended care plan, you create the foundation for implementing your financial strategy and ensuring your care preferences are honored.

These legal documents serve as the voice of your values and wishes if you become unable to express them directly, providing both protection and peace of mind for you and your loved ones.

☑ ACTION STEPS CHECKLIST

All worksheets and templates for this book are online at
WWW.YOURRETIREMENTBLINDSPOT.COM/RESOURCES
Complete them as digital forms or download PDFs. Scan the QR code here:

1. Review your existing legal documents with long-term care specifically in mind. Do they address incapacity planning beyond end-of-life concerns?

2. Create a personal care plan documenting your preferences for daily routines, living environment, and quality-of-life considerations.

3. Discuss with potential agents their willingness and ability to serve in various roles (financial power of attorney, healthcare agent, trustee).

4. Schedule a consultation with an elder law attorney to update or create documents tailored to your long-term care plan.

5. Establish a regular review schedule (every 3-5 years or after major life changes) for all legal documents.

SPECIAL PLANNING SITUATIONS

Long-term care planning isn't one-size-fits-all. Your marital status, family situation, and business interests require specialized approaches.

This section addresses unique planning considerations for couples, singles, business owners, and those coordinating long-term care with broader financial plans.

COUPLES PLANNING

- *Strategic considerations for joint vs. individual coverage*

- *Maximizing discounts and shared benefits*

- *Preparing for the financial impact of widowhood*

- *Finding common ground when spouses have different perspectives*

COUPLES PLANNING: PROTECTING EACH OTHER AND YOUR LEGACY

Long-term care planning for couples involves a fundamentally different calculus than individual planning. You're not just protecting assets—you're protecting each other. The decisions you make together determine not only your financial security but the well-being of the surviving spouse and the legacy you leave behind.

The challenge extends beyond the technical: Should you pursue joint or individual coverage? How do you maximize shared benefits while maintaining flexibility? What happens to the surviving spouse's financial security if one of you needs years of care?

These are strategic questions, but they're also deeply personal. Couples rarely approach long-term care planning from the same perspective. One spouse may have witnessed a parent's decline and feels urgency. The other may have seen a relative live independently into their nineties and questions the need for coverage at all. Different risk tolerances, family experiences, and financial philosophies create tension that no illustration or spreadsheet can resolve.

The goal isn't to eliminate these differences. It's to build a plan that honors both perspectives while ensuring neither spouse becomes a financial or caregiving burden to the other. That requires understanding the unique strategic considerations couples face and finding common ground even when you start from very different places.

NAVIGATOR STORY

FREYA AND ANDERS – FINDING COMMON GROUND

When Freya and Anders sat down for their first long-term care planning conversation, they quickly realized they had very different perspectives.

Anders, an engineer who had watched his father's savings deplete during a lengthy nursing home stay, wanted comprehensive coverage with all the available bells and whistles. Freya, whose mother had lived independently until her death at 94, questioned whether they needed any coverage at all.

They spent three meetings just getting on the same page. But once they understood this wasn't just about protecting their assets but about protecting each other, everything changed.

"I didn't want Anders lying awake at night worried about taking care of me," Freya explains. "And he didn't want me spending my eighties managing his care and depleting everything we'd built."

Their final plan reflected both their concerns: a joint hybrid policy that covered both of them with a shared pool of benefits. If either needed care, they could access the full benefit amount. If neither of them needed care, the policy provided a death benefit to their heirs.

"The joint policy gave us both what we needed," Anders explains. "I got comprehensive protection, and Freya appreciated that we weren't paying for two separate policies when we might only need one."

"Once we stopped debating if we needed coverage and started talking about what would actually protect both of us, the decision became clear," Freya adds.

STRATEGIC COVERAGE CONSIDERATIONS

For couples, the first major decision is whether to pursue joint or individual coverage. This isn't merely a financial calculation but a strategic choice that should reflect your health profiles, age difference, and relationship dynamics.

Evaluating Joint vs. Individual Coverage

Joint coverage, often structured as "shared care" in traditional policies or as a single policy with two insureds in hybrid policies, offers several advantages. Most notably, it creates a pool of benefits that either spouse can access, effectively increasing the resources available to the spouse who needs more care.

> **BOTTOM LINE:** Joint coverage doesn't necessarily mean a single policy. It can mean two individual policies with a shared care rider, or a single policy covering two lives. The right structure depends on your age difference, health profiles, and financial objectives.

Consider the case of a hypothetical couple, Aaron and Miriam Rosenberg: With a seven-year age difference and significantly different health profiles, individual policies made more sense despite the slightly higher combined premium.

They realized that if they went with a joint policy, Miriam's health issues might have disqualified both. By applying separately, Aaron qualified for preferred rates while Miriam still obtained standard coverage.

When evaluating joint versus individual coverage, consider:

- **Health Disparities:** If one spouse has significant health concerns, individual applications may prevent those issues from affecting the healthier spouse's eligibility or rates.

- **Age Differences:** Couples with substantial age differences may find individual policies more cost-effective, as the younger spouse's premiums would increase significantly in a joint policy.

- **Benefit Flexibility:** Joint policies typically offer more flexibility in how benefits are used between spouses, which can be valuable if care needs are likely to be uneven.

- **Relationship Dynamics:** For blended families or second marriages, individual policies may better align with estate planning goals for respective children.

While many couples find value in shared or joint benefits for the flexibility they provide, this approach requires careful consideration. A significant risk exists if one spouse develops a long-duration condition like Alzheimer's disease and uses most or all of the shared benefit pool, potentially leaving the surviving spouse without sufficient coverage.

It's worth noting that some carriers offer lifetime benefits for couples. For example, OneAmerica's Asset Care offers unlimited benefits for both spouses through a hybrid policy, combining LTC coverage with a death benefit.

In cases where lifetime coverage is available for both spouses, a joint policy may be particularly advantageous, as it addresses the concern of one spouse depleting the benefit pool.

The decision between joint and individual coverage should ultimately be based on each couple's unique health histories, family longevity patterns, available carrier options, and overall financial resources dedicated to extended care planning.[98]

Leveraging Discounts and Shared Benefits

Most carriers offer "couples discounts" ranging from 10% to 30%, even when spouses purchase individual policies. These discounts acknowledge the built-in support system that married couples provide, which typically results in shorter claim periods.

> **KEY POINT:** Always ask about all available discount options and carefully evaluate whether shared benefits align with your specific situation, considering factors such as health histories, family longevity patterns, and overall financial resources.

These discounts often apply even if only one spouse purchases coverage, though usually at a reduced percentage. Some carriers extend these discounts to domestic partners, siblings living together, or other multi-life situations.

For traditional long-term care insurance, shared benefit riders create additional value but require careful consideration. These riders allow spouses to access each other's benefit pools if their own becomes depleted. For example, if each spouse purchases a three-year benefit period with a shared care rider, they create a combined six-year pool that either can access.

While this provides protection when one spouse needs significantly more care than the other, it also creates the risk that one spouse with a long-duration condition could deplete most or all of the shared resources.

Some carriers have addressed this concern with innovative approaches, such as National Guardian Life's "third pool" shared care benefit, which provides additional protection beyond individual benefit accounts.[99]

With asset-based or hybrid policies, the approach differs slightly. Some policies offer joint-options where a single policy covers both spouses, often with a shared pool of benefits. The advantage here is simplicity—one policy, one premium, one set of benefits to track—but the trade-off can be less flexibility in benefit customization.

NAVIGATOR STORY

THE JOHNSONS' ASSET-BASED CARE STRATEGY

When Ellen and Robert Johnson were in their mid-50s, they chose a hybrid long-term care policy with shared coverage—one policy designed to protect both of them.

More than twenty years later, at age 76, Ellen needed care for several months after a stroke. Their policy provided a shared pool of benefits, covering Ellen's care expenses without impacting their retirement savings.

"Because we chose a joint hybrid policy, Ellen was able to receive the care she needed, and we still have coverage left if I ever need care—or if Ellen needs care again in the future," Robert explains. "Even after a claim, any unused benefits remain available for either of us, or, depending on what's left, as a reduced tax-free death benefit for our children."

Their decision to leverage a hybrid policy gave them peace of mind, knowing their plan could adapt to whatever the future holds.

PREPARING FOR LIFE ALONE:
THE WIDOW'S PENALTY

Perhaps the most overlooked aspect of couples planning is preparing for what financial professionals often call "the widow's penalty"—the financial challenges that occur when one spouse dies.

This penalty manifests in several ways:

- **Income Reduction:** When one spouse dies, household income often decreases significantly due to the loss of the smaller of two Social Security benefits and potentially a portion of pension income.[100]

- **Tax Bracket Changes:** The surviving spouse files as a single taxpayer rather than married filing jointly, potentially pushing them into a higher tax bracket despite having lower income.

- **Healthcare Cost Increases:** Medicare premiums may increase for the surviving spouse based on their individual income rather than joint income.

- **Long-term Care Burden:** The surviving spouse loses their primary caregiver, increasing the likelihood they'll need paid care services.

BOTTOM LINE: The death of a spouse creates both an income shock and a potential care crisis for the survivor. Effective long-term care planning must account for this vulnerability.

Long-term care planning can address this vulnerability in several ways:

- **Income Protection:** Covering care costs through insurance rather than depleting income helps protect the financial security of the surviving spouse.

- **Asset Preservation:** Preserving assets through insurance coverage significantly improves the surviving spouse's potential for maintaining financial independence.

- **Care Coordination Benefits:** Many policies include care coordination services that become especially valuable for a widow or widower navigating care decisions alone.

- **Death Benefits:** Hybrid policies include a death benefit that can provide a lump sum to beneficiaries, often including the surviving spouse, if long-term care benefits are not fully used. Some joint policies allow the surviving spouse to continue coverage or receive a portion of the remaining death benefit, offering added financial security.[101]

Research from the Social Security Administration shows that women face significant financial challenges after widowhood, with household income often declining substantially due to the loss of Social Security or pension benefits, while expenses such as housing remain relatively stable, increasing the risk of poverty.[102]

Given that women typically outlive men and are more likely to need extended care, this planning aspect is especially critical.[103]

FINDING COMMON GROUND WHEN PERSPECTIVES DIFFER

It's remarkably common for spouses to have different views on extended care planning. These differences often stem from:

- **Different Family Experiences:** One spouse may have witnessed the realities of providing long-term care for a parent while the other has not.

- **Risk Tolerance Disparities:** Spouses frequently have different comfort levels with financial risk.

- **Health Awareness Gaps:** One spouse may be more attuned to health vulnerabilities than the other.

- **Caregiving Expectations:** Unspoken assumptions about who would provide care can create planning conflicts.

When spouses disagree about extended care planning, the following approach can help find common ground:

1. **Share Personal Experiences and Concerns:** Begin by understanding each other's perspectives. Often, resistance to planning stems from fear or misconceptions rather than rational analysis. Create a judgment-free space to share concerns.

2. **Focus on Protecting Each Other, Not Just Assets:** Frame the conversation around protecting each other rather than protecting money. Research shows that 61% of caregivers are women, and the physical and emotional toll of caregiving can be substantial.[104] Discussing how proper planning protects both spouses from this burden often resonates more deeply than financial arguments.

3. **Consider a Phased Approach:** If one spouse remains reluctant, consider starting with a modest plan that can be enhanced later. Some coverage is better than none, and taking that first step often leads to greater comfort with the concept over time.

4. **Engage a Neutral Third Party:** Sometimes an objective professional can help bridge the gap between differing perspectives. Financial advisors, elder law attorneys, or certified long-term care specialists can provide education without the emotional charge that sometimes accompanies spousal discussions.

NAVIGATOR STORY

FINDING MIDDLE GROUND

After 25 years of marriage, Nia and Omar found themselves at odds over long-term care planning.

Omar, a 55-year-old physician, wanted comprehensive long-term care protection. Nia, who had recently helped her own mother manage care needs at home, believed they could self-fund and rely on family if necessary.

Their breakthrough came when their advisor suggested a hybrid policy. "The return of premium feature and the guaranteed death benefit gave me the security I needed," Nia explains. "And Omar got the long-term care protection he wanted. We both felt heard."

☑ ACTION STEPS CHECKLIST

All worksheets and templates for this book are online at
WWW.YOURRETIREMENTBLINDSPOT.COM/RESOURCES
Complete them as digital forms or download PDFs. Scan the QR code here:

1. Evaluate your health profiles together to determine whether joint or individual coverage makes more sense for your situation.

2. Calculate the financial impact of widowhood on the surviving spouse, including income changes, tax implications, and potential care needs.

3. Document each spouse's care preferences using the "Care Preferences Assessment" worksheet, then discuss areas of alignment and difference.

4. Meet with a financial professional who specializes in long-term care planning to explore options that address both spouses' concerns.

5. Review your existing estate planning documents to ensure they complement your long-term care strategy and protect the surviving spouse.

SINGLE PERSON PLANNING

- *Creating a robust support network without family caregivers*
- *Understanding the unique financial considerations for solo agers*
- *Working effectively with professional care managers*
- *Developing meaningful legacy plans without direct descendants*

DESIGNING YOUR OWN SAFETY NET

Consider the fictitious example of Patricia Reynolds. She retired at 67, she had a successful career, a comfortable nest egg, and an active social life—but no spouse or children.

She found that everyone kept asking who would take care of her if she needed help. She found it frustrating because they assumed she hadn't thought about it, when in fact she had a more detailed plan than most of her married friends.

Patricia represents a growing demographic: the solo ager. Whether never married, divorced, widowed, or without children, approximately 28% of Americans over 65 live alone.[105]

For these individuals, long-term care planning isn't optional. It's essential.

Elder law attorneys agree: The biggest mistake singles make isn't failing to plan. It's assuming the planning process is identical to that of couples.

In reality, solo agers face unique challenges. Without a spouse or adult children to rely on, singles often need different legal documents, such as carefully crafted powers of attorney and advance directives, as well as a more robust professional support network.

Proactive planning can help ensure that their wishes are honored and that they have trusted advocates in place if extended care is ever needed.

BUILDING YOUR SUPPORT NETWORK

For married couples, the default caregiver is typically the spouse, with adult children providing secondary support. Singles must be more intentional about creating their care team, starting long before care is needed.

Creating Your Care Circle

The most effective support networks for singles combine trusted friends, extended family, and professionals into what gerontologists call a "care circle."

This approach recognizes that while one friend or family member cannot provide the comprehensive support a spouse typically would, a thoughtfully assembled team can collectively meet those needs.

> **BOTTOM LINE:** The time to build your care circle is now, not when you're in crisis. Nurturing these relationships during healthy years creates the foundation for support when you need it most.

Your care circle might include:

- **Trusted Friends:** Often the first line of support for singles, close friends can provide emotional support, help with transportation, or check in regularly. However, friends typically have their own families and may face similar age-related challenges of their own, limiting their availability as long-term caregivers.

- **Extended Family:** Nieces, nephews, cousins, or siblings may be willing to help with oversight or occasional support, though they may not be geographically close or available for daily assistance.

- **Neighbors:** Proximity makes neighbors valuable for quick check-ins or emergency response, especially in senior-friendly communities where neighbors understand the importance of looking out for one another.

- **Faith Community:** Religious organizations often have formal or informal support systems for members, from regular visitation to volunteer transportation services.

 **Professional Connections:** Former colleagues, your attorney, financial advisor, certified long-term care specialist, or medical professionals can form part of your extended support network.

The key is to be explicit about your expectations and their willingness to help.

Experts agree that singles who proactively build a support network through direct conversations are better prepared for future care needs than those who rely on assumptions.[106]

NAVIGATOR STORY

A NEW BEGINNING, A NEW PLAN

After a late-in-life divorce at 65, Keisha found herself navigating retirement alone. Recognizing the importance of having a reliable support system, she began intentionally building her care circle.

She became more active in her church and neighborhood association, joined a local book club and reconnected with her cousins and longtime friends.

"I keep a contact list of my care circle on my refrigerator and update it every year," Keisha explains. "Everyone on that list has agreed to be part of my support system and knows who else is involved. It's not just about having people to call in an emergency. It's about creating a community that will notice if something's wrong."

The Professional Care Manager: Your Essential Advocate

For singles, a professional care manager often becomes the linchpin of an effective extended care plan.

> **KEY POINT:** Interview potential care managers while you're healthy. Look for someone who listens well, respects your preferences, and has deep knowledge of local resources. The relationship works best when established before a crisis.

These professionals, typically nurses or social workers with specialized gerontology training, serve as navigators through the complex healthcare and long-term care systems.

Many financial planners and elder care experts agree: a good care manager is the closest thing to having an adult child advocating for you.

They know the local resources, can coordinate between different providers, and most importantly, they are professionally obligated to put your interests first.

Care managers provide services that friends or distant family members often cannot:

- **Needs Assessment:** Evaluating your physical, cognitive, and emotional status to determine appropriate care levels.

- **Care Coordination:** Managing communication between healthcare providers, caregivers, and other professionals.

- **Provider Selection:** Identifying and vetting appropriate care providers based on your specific needs and preferences.

- **Crisis Intervention:** Responding quickly when health status changes or care arrangements break down.

- **Ongoing Monitoring:** Regularly evaluating care quality and adjusting plans as needs evolve.

Many traditional and hybrid long-term care insurance policies include valuable care coordination benefits that can connect you with these professionals when needed.

For singles without such coverage, professional care managers typically charge $800 to $2,000 for initial assessments, depending on the region, with ongoing services ranging from $90 to $250 per hour or monthly retainer fees.

Additional costs, such as mileage, and/or travel time may apply, so it's important to confirm billing details and secure written agreements before starting services.

Medicare, Medicaid, Medigap, and most Medicare Advantage plans do not cover these services, though some long-term care insurance policies may partially offset costs.[107]

FINANCIAL CONSIDERATIONS UNIQUE TO SOLO AGERS

Singles face distinct financial challenges in extended care planning that couples don't encounter:[108]

- **No Economies of Scale:** Singles bear the full cost of housing, utilities, and basic expenses without the sharing that benefits couples.

- **No Spousal Safety Net:** Singles lack the built-in caregiver that married people often have, potentially necessitating paid care earlier and for longer periods.

- **Income Replacement Challenges:** Without a spouse's income to help cover costs, singles must ensure their own resources can fully fund both regular expenses and care costs.

- **Higher Relative Insurance Costs:** While premiums for singles are lower than for couples combined, the per-person cost is typically higher without couples discounts.

These factors make proactive financial planning particularly important for singles. Consider these strategies:

Liquidity Planning

Singles need more accessible assets than couples because care needs could require immediate funding without a spouse to manage financial matters.

Financial experts suggest that singles maintain a more robust liquidity strategy than the standard emergency fund. A prudent approach involves setting aside dedicated cash reserves to cover the initial, out-of-pocket costs of starting care, which can easily run into thousands of dollars for assessments, deposits, and home modifications.

Without a spouse to handle logistics, singles often need to pay for services that couples might manage themselves. This proactive approach helps ensure that funds are readily available for emergencies, the sudden onset of care needs, and the costs associated with moving between care settings.[109]

Income Stream Protection

For singles, protecting income streams is paramount since there's no secondary income to fall back on.

Consider these strategies to ensure your essential expenses are covered, even during periods of incapacity or health crisis:

- **Annuitizing a Portion of Assets:** Consider converting a portion of your savings into a lifetime annuity can provide guaranteed income that continues regardless of market conditions or health status.

- **Leveraging Social Security Optimization:** Delaying Social Security benefits can increase your monthly income for life, providing a larger, inflation-adjusted base.

- **Emphasizing Dividend and Interest-Producing Investments:** Allocating assets to dividend-paying stocks, bonds, or other income-generating vehicles can help maintain cash flow without requiring active management.

- **Implementing Systematic Withdrawal Plans:** Setting up automatic, scheduled withdrawals from retirement accounts can help ensure a steady flow of income.

- **Establishing Automatic Bill Payment Systems:** Automating payments for essential expenses ensures bills are paid on time, even if you're unable to manage finances directly.

- **Maintaining Sufficient Liquid Reserves:** Keeping an accessible cash reserve can help bridge gaps during transitions or emergencies.

- **Annuities with Income Riders and Enhanced Withdrawal Features:** Some annuities offer income riders that increase withdrawals if you experience chronic illness or confinement. While these features can help supplement income during a care event, they do not provide comprehensive long-term care coverage or meet state and federal long-term care insurance definitions.[110]

Long-Term Care Insurance Considerations

While the basic insurance options remain the same for singles as for couples, the selection criteria often differ.

Singles typically benefit most from policies that emphasize:

- **Home Care Benefits:** Since singles are more likely to need paid home care earlier in their care journey, robust home care coverage is essential.

- **Care Coordination Services:** Look for policies with strong care coordination benefits that help arrange and monitor care services.

- **Shorter Elimination Periods:** Without a spouse to provide care during the waiting period, shorter elimination periods often make sense despite the higher premium.

- **Longer Benefit Period:** Consider a minimum of 4 years or, if manageable financially, a lifetime benefit.

- **Inflation Protection:** Singles, especially women, tend to have longer care needs, making inflation protection particularly valuable.

Research from the American Association for Long-Term Care Insurance shows that single women file more claims and have longer claim periods than either married women or men of any marital status.[111] This makes comprehensive coverage particularly important for single women, despite the higher premiums they typically face.

LEGACY PLANNING WITHOUT DIRECT DESCENDANTS

For singles without children, legacy planning takes on different dimensions. Rather than focusing primarily on efficient wealth transfer to the next generation, singles often seek to:

- **Support Extended Family:** Many singles choose to benefit nieces, nephews, or other relatives.

- **Further Charitable Causes:** Creating a lasting impact through charitable giving.

- **Leave a Living Legacy:** Establishing programs or foundations that reflect personal values.

- **Protect Beloved Pets:** Ensuring continued care for animal companions.

The key is aligning your legacy planning with your extended care strategy to ensure that your wishes are honored regardless of health status.

> **BOTTOM LINE:** Without children to advocate for your wishes, documenting your intentions clearly and creating the legal framework to support them becomes even more critical.

Essential Documents for Singles

While everyone needs basic estate planning documents, singles should pay particular attention to:

- **Durable Power of Attorney:** This document becomes especially critical for singles, as there's no spouse with automatic legal standing to manage affairs. Consider naming multiple agents with clear succession.

- **Healthcare Proxy:** Designate someone who understands your healthcare values and will advocate for your wishes. Geographic proximity matters more for singles than for those with spouses.

- **HIPAA Authorization:** Include multiple trusted individuals to ensure someone can access your medical information when needed.

- **Revocable Living Trust:** More important for singles than couples, a properly funded trust can provide seamless management of assets during incapacity without court intervention.

- **Pet Trust or Care Agreement:** Formal arrangements for pet care are particularly important for singles, as pets may otherwise end up in shelters if their owner requires facility care.

Attorney and elder law experts recommend that singles review these documents annually. Without a spouse who is naturally aware of your changing circumstances, it's easy for these documents to become outdated.

Many attorneys suggest calendaring an annual review date, perhaps your birthday, to ensure your documents still reflect your current wishes and relationships.

 **NAVIGATOR STORY**

SECURING INDEPENDENCE AND LEGACY

As a single woman with no children, Dr. Dana Hoffman, a successful retired educator, faced a dual challenge: how to fund potential long-term care needs without a spouse's support, and how to ensure her significant estate would fulfill her lifelong commitment to education.

Working with her certified financial advisor and an experienced estate planning attorney, she created a plan that used a hybrid long-term care policy to create a dedicated, leveraged pool of money for her care.

She placed the policy and other assets into a revocable living trust, designed to ensure the policy's benefits could be used for her care, naming a licensed professional fiduciary as the successor trustee to manage her affairs if she becomes unable.

"My biggest fear was that my legacy would be dismantled to pay for my care, or that there would be no one I trusted to manage things," Dana explains. "This structure protects me first, ensuring I have the funds for quality care. The trust ensures my wishes are carried out precisely, directing my estate to establish a scholarship fund for education. Knowing that my life's work is secure, no matter what happens to my health, gives me true independence."

☑ ACTION STEPS CHECKLIST

All worksheets and templates for this book are online at
WWW.YOURRETIREMENTBLINDSPOT.COM/RESOURCES
Complete them as digital forms or download PDFs. Scan the QR code here:

1. Create a contact list of your current support network, identifying gaps that might need to be filled with professional services.

2. Interview at least two professional care managers in your area to understand their services and establish a relationship before you need assistance.

3. Review your emergency fund strategy to ensure you have adequate liquidity for potential care transitions.

4. Evaluate your insurance options with particular attention to home care benefits and care coordination services.

5. Update your essential legal documents and schedule an annual review to keep them current with your changing relationships and preferences.

BUSINESS OWNER CONSIDERATIONS

- *Identifying the critical protection gap that disability insurance does not cover*

- *Leveraging your business entity for tax-deductible premiums and tax-free benefits*

- *Closing the succession planning loophole by adding a long-term care trigger to your buy-sell agreement*

- *Using executive carve-out plans as a strategic tool to retain your most valuable talent*

THE PROTECTION GAP MOST BUSINESS OWNERS MISS

As a business owner, your company represents a unique planning opportunity that extends beyond traditional business considerations.

You've likely secured it against your death with life insurance and protected your income from a disability. But a critical blind spot remains: the risk of needing long-term custodial care.

This isn't about replacing your paycheck. Disability insurance answers the question, "How do we replace my income if I can't work?" Long-term care planning answers a different, more complex question: "How do we pay for my care without jeopardizing the business?"

NAVIGATOR STORY

BEYOND DISABILITY PROTECTION

Arthur Vance, founder of a successful logistics company, believed he had an ironclad plan. He had key person insurance, a funded buy-sell agreement, and robust disability coverage for himself.

But when a severe stroke at 68 left him needing years of custodial assistance, his plan revealed a fatal flaw.

His disability policy replaced his income as designed, but it was never intended to cover the high cost of his actual care.

"My disability insurance was a lifesaver for my personal income," Arthur explains, "but it did nothing to stop my health crisis from becoming a business crisis. We had to siphon cash flow meant for new equipment to cover my $8,000 monthly care costs. Worse, it pulled my daughter, our COO, away from running the company to coordinate my care. We didn't just lose capital; we lost leadership when we needed it most."

Arthur's story highlights a critical challenge for business owners. By incorporating long-term care planning, such as hybrid policies and care coordination, you can protect both your personal care needs and your business's financial stability.

OPTIMIZING BUSINESS STRUCTURES FOR LONG-TERM CARE

As a business owner, you have unique opportunities to leverage your company structure for long-term care planning.

The approach varies significantly based on your business entity type, ownership arrangement, and long-term goals.

Strategic Tax Advantages by Business Entity

Different business structures offer distinct planning opportunities, with C-Corporations being the gold standard, providing the most powerful tax advantages:

C-Corporations

C-Corporations offer unmatched tax advantages for long-term care planning. As separate tax entities, C-Corps can deduct 100% of the long-term care insurance premium component for tax-qualified policies as a business expense under IRC §162(a), with no age-based limits—a significant advantage over all other business structures. This includes coverage for owner-employees, their spouses, and tax dependents.

Under IRC §106, the LTC premiums paid by the corporation are excluded from the employee's gross income and are not subject to federal income tax withholding, Social Security, Medicare, or unemployment taxes.[112]

C-Corps are also not subject to discrimination rules for tax-qualified long-term care insurance, allowing them to selectively offer coverage to a valid class of employees—such as executives or key personnel—through executive carve-out plans.

S-Corporations

Shareholders who own more than 2% of an S-Corporation must include the premium value in their income. However, they can then deduct a portion of these premiums as an above-the-line self-employed health insurance deduction, reducing adjusted gross income without itemizing. The deduction is subject to IRS age-based limits, which cap the deductible amount based on the insured's age.[113]

Partnerships and LLC Members

Partners and LLC members treated as partners for tax purposes follow similar rules to S-Corporation shareholders. The partnership can pay the premiums, which are reported as guaranteed payments to partners, who then may claim an above-the-line self-employed health insurance deduction, reducing adjusted gross income. Like S-Corps, these deductions are subject to age-based limits.[114] [115]

Sole Proprietors

Sole proprietors can deduct a portion of their long-term care insurance premiums as an above-the-line self-employed health insurance deduction, reducing adjusted gross income without itemizing. The deduction is subject to IRS age-based limits based on the insured's age.[116] [117]

Age-Based Deduction Limits

The age-based premium deduction limits for self-employed individuals increase with age, recognizing that premiums typically rise as you get older. For 2026, these limits range from $500 for those 40 and under to $6,200 for those over 70.[118]

While these limits may cover only a portion of actual premium costs, they provide valuable tax relief that isn't available to most employees.

BOTTOM LINE: The tax treatment of long-term care insurance premiums follows a consistent above-the-line structure across business entities, with C-Corporations enjoying uncapped deductions and pass-through entities subject to age-based limits. For hybrid policies, only the long-term care portion is deductible if separately identifiable. Consulting with both your tax advisor and a long-term care specialist ensures you maximize available deductions.

Disclaimer: This information is for educational purposes only and should not be considered tax advice. Tax laws are complex and subject to change. Consult with a qualified tax professional regarding your specific situation.

Using Long-Term Care Benefits to Attract and Retain Talent

Key employees, especially those in their 50s, are constantly being recruited by competitors offering more money. When you're competing for talent, long-term care benefits can be the differentiator that makes someone think twice before taking a competitor's offer.

Why This Beats a Cash Bonus

Cash bonuses are nice, but temporary. They get taxed heavily, losing 20-40% right off the top, and what's left often gets absorbed into lifestyle expenses. They don't create lasting loyalty or solve a deep-seated worry. Business-paid long-term care coverage hits differently. It addresses a core fear that many key employees have as they enter their 50s and 60s: the specific, nagging anxiety that healthcare costs, especially long-term care, could completely wipe out everything they've saved, or worse, turn them into a financial and caregiving burden on their children.

Strategic Value

When structured properly, these benefits can be paid up before the employee retires, locking in guaranteed coverage for life. This demonstrates a company's commitment to an employee's long-term well-being, not just quarterly performance. For executives who have watched their own parents struggle with care costs, this benefit can be the deciding factor in choosing one employer over another.

Disclaimer: This information is for educational purposes only. Executive benefit programs must comply with applicable tax and employment laws. Consult with qualified legal, tax, and benefits professionals regarding your specific situation.

NAVIGATOR STORY

THE EXECUTIVE CARVE-OUT

Claire Sterling, CEO of SterlingTech, a C-Corporation in the growing tech industry, noticed her company was losing key executives to competitors.

To enhance retention, she implemented an executive carve-out plan for all director-level employees and above. Under this plan, SterlingTech paid premiums for personally owned hybrid long-term care policies, with the premiums fully deductible to the corporation as a business expense.

The tax treatment was highly favorable: The long-term care premium portion was excluded from the employees' gross income. Only the life insurance portion was taxable to the employees. To neutralize this tax impact, the company provided additional compensation to cover the employees' tax liability on the life insurance component, ensuring the benefit was truly cost-free to the executives. Benefits would be received tax-free when used for qualified care expenses.

"It was a game-changer for retention," Claire explains. "Several executives told me they'd been approached by competitors offering higher salaries, but our long-term care benefit was something their families valued too much to leave behind. It showed them we were invested in their long-term well-being, not just their quarterly performance."

SUCCESSION PLANNING THAT PROTECTS YOUR LIFE'S WORK

For many business owners, their company represents not just their largest asset but their life's work and legacy.

An owner's extended care event can trigger a cascade of threats to the company's survival, making integrated succession planning essential.

Without a plan, an owner's care needs can jeopardize business continuity by:

- **Forcing Liquidation:** Requiring the sale of business assets or the entire company to pay for care, often at distressed prices.

- **Creating a Leadership Vacuum:** An owner's cognitive or physical decline can leave the business rudderless if a transition plan isn't in place.

- **Igniting Family Conflicts:** Intersecting business interests and care needs can cause deep disagreements, particularly in family-owned businesses.

- **Undermining Client Confidence:** An owner's extended absence without a clear leadership transition can cause customers to lose faith and take their business elsewhere.

> **KEY POINT:** A buy-sell agreement without a specific trigger for a long-term care event is an incomplete succession plan. It leaves your business vulnerable to the exact risks you're trying to prevent. Consult attorneys to customize triggers for your business. Consult state-specific attorneys for agreement terms.

Crucially, these threats often emerge gradually. Cognitive decline can impair business judgment long before triggering traditional disability benefits, making a documented succession plan the only reliable safeguard for your life's work.

The Buy-Sell Agreement: Your Cornerstone for Continuity

The cornerstone of this integrated planning is the buy-sell agreement. While these legal contracts typically address death, disability, or retirement, many fail to adequately plan for long-term care needs.

Business attorneys note that traditional disability triggers in buy-sell agreements often miss the gray area where an owner isn't fully disabled but is experiencing cognitive decline that harms the business.

Many attorneys now recommend including specific extended care triggers in these agreements, defining how a care need is determined and what happens when that trigger is met.

Insurance provides the most efficient funding mechanism for these agreements. Life insurance funds buyouts upon death, while a separate qualified long-term care insurance policy ensures tax-advantaged benefits to cover care needs, protecting the business and the owner's family from potential high costs of extended care.

NAVIGATOR STORY

THE SUCCESSION SAFETY NET

Lukas Schmidt and Alex Voss, partners at Schmidt-Voss Enterprises, discovered during a five-year review that their buy-sell agreement covered death and disability but ignored a potential long, slow decline. With professional counsel, they amended the agreement to add an objective incapacity trigger tied to a physician's certification of cognitive impairment or chronic illness, in addition to the existing death/disability provisions.

They funded the plan with two separate policies in a cross-purchase structure—each partner owning a life insurance policy and a qualified long-term care policy on the other—to cover care needs and provide liquidity for a death-triggered buyout. The partnership paid the premiums, with tax treatment coordinated as part of their compensation/distribution planning (CPA-reviewed).

Five years later, Lukas was diagnosed with early-onset Alzheimer's. The long-term care policy delivered tax-free benefits for his care per the policy terms, while the partnership funded the buyout through installment payments per the agreed valuation formula. "It was the hardest conversation of my life, but the easiest business decision—because we had already made it," Alex said. "The defined trigger removed ambiguity and conflict, protecting Lukas' family and the company's continuity."

Disclaimer: This material is for educational purposes only and not legal or tax advice. Consult qualified counsel and a CPA to draft agreement terms and determine tax treatment.

When Business and Personal Planning Intersect

For business owners, the line between business and personal planning often blurs. This intersection creates both challenges and opportunities that require thoughtful coordination.

Balancing Business and Personal Assets

Many business owners have a disproportionate amount of their wealth tied up in their business, representing the majority of their net worth.

This concentration creates unique extended care planning challenges:

- **Liquidity Constraints:** Business equity, while valuable, isn't readily accessible for care expenses without disrupting operations.

- **Valuation Uncertainties:** Business valuations fluctuate based on market conditions, industry trends, and leadership stability.

- **Tax Implications:** Converting business assets to cash for care expenses often triggers significant tax consequences.

These challenges make insurance-based solutions particularly valuable. Think of long-term care insurance as a firewall protecting your company from your personal health risks.

Without this dedicated funding source, your business becomes your long-term care plan by default—a role it was never designed to fill.

Integrated Planning Strategies

The most effective approach integrates business and personal long-term care planning through several key strategies:

- **Maximize Your Entity's Tax Advantages:** Understand how your current business structure treats long-term care premiums and benefits, then design your coverage to capture maximum tax efficiency. As mentioned, C-Corporations offer the most powerful advantages, but every entity type provides meaningful benefits when structured properly.

- **Compensation Planning:** Structure compensation to maximize deductibility of extended care premiums while minimizing tax impact on key employees and owners.

- **Multiple-Purpose Solutions:** Consider hybrid long-term care policies that provide tax-free long-term care benefits for care needs, with a tax-free life insurance death benefit available for family or business succession needs if long-term care benefits are unused or partially used.

- **Coordinated Legal Documents:** Ensure your business continuity documents align with your personal advance directives and powers of attorney. If you become incapacitated, both your business and personal affairs need clear decision-making authority.

This integration requires collaboration among your advisors. Your long-term care specialist, financial advisor, business attorney, and CPA should work together to create a cohesive strategy that protects both your business and personal interests.

BOTTOM LINE: For business owners, personal health planning and business succession planning are not separate disciplines—they are two sides of the same coin. A failure to plan for one almost guarantees the failure of the other.

Family Business Considerations

Nowhere are these challenges more acute than in a family business. Here, the lines between shareholder, employee, and family member completely dissolve.

Without a documented plan for a long-term care event, adult children are forced into an impossible choice: manage the business or manage their parent's care.

This conflict between professional duty and family loyalty is a primary source of the bitter disputes that can fracture a family, sometimes permanently.

Clear, documented planning is not just about business continuity; it's about preserving the family itself.

NAVIGATOR STORY

THE CASTELLANOS FAMILY — WHEN DUTY DIVIDES

Robert Castellano spent thirty-five years building Castellano Construction into a regional powerhouse, employing forty people and generating $8 million in annual revenue. His daughter Maria served as CFO, his son Vincent ran operations, and his youngest daughter Elena managed client relations.

When Robert suffered a stroke at 68, the carefully balanced family business began to fracture.

Maria immediately stepped in to manage her father's care—coordinating physical therapy, handling medical appointments, and eventually overseeing round-the-clock home health aides as his condition deteriorated. Vincent assumed she'd continue managing the company's finances remotely. Elena expected her to share caregiving responsibilities.

Neither happened.

"I was spending 30 hours a week on Dad's care," Maria explains. "I couldn't review contracts, approve payroll, or handle vendor negotiations. Vincent was furious because projects were stalling. Elena resented that I'd 'abandoned' the family by not being at the hospital every day."

Within six months, the company had lost two major clients due to cash flow issues Maria would have caught earlier. Vincent considered leaving to start his own firm. Elena stopped speaking to Maria entirely.

"The tragedy wasn't Dad's stroke," Vincent says now. "It was that we had no plan for what would happen if he couldn't run the business. We spent more time arguing about who was abandoning their duty than we did figuring out how to keep the company—and our family—intact."

The Castellanos eventually sold the business at a significant loss. Robert's care consumed most of the proceeds. The siblings haven't shared a holiday meal in four years.

"Dad built something that was supposed to bring us together," Elena reflects. "Instead, it tore us apart. And the worst part? It was completely avoidable."

☑ ACTION STEPS CHECKLIST

All worksheets and templates for this book are online at
WWW.YOURRETIREMENTBLINDSPOT.COM/RESOURCES
Complete them as digital forms or download PDFs. Scan the QR code here:

1. Review your business structure with your tax advisor to determine the most advantageous approach for long-term care premium deductibility.

2. Evaluate your buy-sell agreement to ensure it adequately addresses long-term care scenarios, particularly cognitive impairment.

3. Consider implementing an executive benefit program that includes long-term care coverage for yourself and key employees.

4. Create a written business continuity plan that specifically addresses who assumes which responsibilities if you require long-term care.

5. Meet with your long-term care specialist, financial advisor, and business attorney together to ensure your business and personal planning strategies are properly aligned.

INTEGRATING LONG-TERM CARE WITH RETIREMENT AND ESTATE PLANNING

- *Why siloed planning fails and integrated strategies succeed*

- *How one financial decision creates unseen chain reactions across your plan*

- *Aligning tax strategies for retirement income, care funding, and legacy goals*

- *Building a collaborative advisory team to protect your family's wealth*

THE INTERCONNECTED PLANNING IMPERATIVE

A well-crafted financial plan is like a high-performance engine, with retirement, estate, and tax planning all working as interconnected parts.

But for many, there's a missing component: long-term care planning.

Treating it as a separate, optional add-on is like installing a critical part with the wrong bolts—under pressure, the entire structure can fail.

NAVIGATOR STORY

THE CO-ORDINATION GAP

Matteo and Daniela, both 72, believed they had comprehensive planning in place. Their financial advisor had structured a retirement income strategy around Matteo's $6,100 monthly pension, their combined Social Security benefits, and a diversified portfolio worth $1.3 million. Their estate attorney had established a revocable trust to avoid probate and minimize estate taxes. Years earlier, they had each purchased traditional long-term care policies from an individual insurance agent.

When Matteo suffered severe spinal injuries after a distracted driver ran a red light and T-boned his car, requiring long-term custodial care after his Medicare skilled care ended, the coordination gaps became apparent. His LTC policy covered facility care, but Daniela wanted him home. The additional home care costs forced portfolio withdrawals that triggered capital gains, pushed more Social Security into taxable range, and consumed assets earmarked for their church.

"Each professional was excellent individually," Daniela reflects, "but no one was looking at how Matteo's care would affect our taxes, our charitable goals, and my retirement security. That coordination gap created a financial chain reaction we never saw coming."

Why Siloed Planning Fails

Matteo and Daniela's experience highlights a fundamental truth: financial planning is an ecosystem. A decision in one area inevitably affects the others. Siloed planning fails because it ignores these critical interactions, leading to:

- **Conflicting Strategies:** A retirement strategy designed for tax-efficient distributions can clash with an extended care need that requires immediate, unplanned withdrawals that disrupt the tax strategy.

- **Unseen Chain Reactions:** For those 65+, liquidating assets to pay for care can increase income enough to trigger IRMAA surcharges—raising Medicare Part B and Part D premiums by hundreds of dollars per month, compounding the cost of self-funding.

- **Medicare Premium Surcharges:** For those 65+, liquidating assets to pay for care can increase income enough to trigger IRMAA surcharges—raising Medicare Part B and Part D premiums by hundreds of dollars per month, compounding the cost of self-funding.

- **Massive Blind Spots:** A retirement plan that models for market risk but ignores the potential multi-hundred-thousand-dollar risk of a long-term care event isn't a complete plan.

Financial professionals consistently observe that clients with integrated planning approaches are significantly more likely to achieve their overall financial goals compared to those with fragmented strategies.

 **BOTTOM LINE:** Integrated planning isn't about making each individual plan perfect; it's about making them work *together*.

The Integration Framework

Effective integration begins with understanding how extended care planning intersects with other key planning areas:

- **Retirement Planning:** Long-term care planning directly affects retirement income sustainability, asset allocation strategies, and withdrawal sequencing.

- **Estate Planning:** Care needs influence wealth transfer timing, asset protection strategies, and legacy preservation approaches.

- **Tax Planning:** Long-term care decisions can have significant tax implications for income, estate, and gift tax exposure.

- **Family Planning:** Care preferences impact family roles, responsibilities, and potential conflicts.

The most successful integrated plans address these intersections proactively rather than reactively.

This means considering potential care scenarios during retirement planning, incorporating care funding strategies into estate plans, and ensuring that tax planning accounts for potential care-related deductions and exclusions.

 **NAVIGATOR STORY**

THE WAKE-UP CALL

David and Melissa Hogan, both 58 and in excellent health, watched with growing concern as David's mother's Alzheimer's disease progressed. Over three years, her memory care facility and home care needs depleted nearly $400,000 of her retirement savings and forced the sale of her cherished vacation property, part of her estate plan for the grandchildren.

"What shocked us wasn't just the cost," David explains. "It was seeing how quickly her carefully constructed estate plan unraveled when faced with long-term care needs."

This experience prompted the Hogans to schedule a joint meeting with their financial advisor and estate planning attorney. "We need to make sure we don't repeat this situation," Melissa told them. "How can we integrate long-term care planning into our existing plans?"

The collaborative review uncovered two critical vulnerabilities: their retirement savings were exposed to long-term care costs without dedicated coverage, and their estate plan lacked protection against asset depletion for care needs. Their advisors worked together to restructure their assets and incorporate hybrid long-term care insurance that complemented both their retirement income strategy and estate plans. This solution would protect their legacy goals while ensuring access to quality care.

"That single meeting was eye-opening," David says. "We're still healthy, but now we have genuine peace of mind knowing our retirement and legacy plans won't collapse if either of us needs care."

TAX PLANNING: THE THREE-DIMENSIONAL CHESS GAME

Perhaps nowhere is integration more critical—or more complex—than in tax planning. Every move, whether paying for care or choosing insurance, affects your income, estate, and legacy across multiple years. Long-term care decisions create tax implications that ripple across income, estate, and gift tax considerations, often spanning multiple tax years and even generations.

Income Tax Considerations

Long-term care expenses and insurance benefits interact with income taxes in several important ways:

- **Medical Expense Deductions:** Qualified long-term care services and eligible insurance premiums can be deducted as medical expenses when they exceed 7.5% of adjusted gross income.[119] This threshold makes timing of expenses and income particularly important in years with significant care costs.

- **Tax-Free Benefits:** Benefits from qualified long-term care insurance policies are generally excluded from income when used for qualified care expenses.[120] This creates a valuable tax advantage compared to using taxable withdrawals from retirement accounts to pay for care.

- **Business Owner Deductions:** As discussed in Chapter 12, business owners may have additional opportunities to deduct premium payments, potentially converting after-tax personal expenses into deductible business expenses.

> **KEY POINT:** Long-term care tax planning requires selecting appropriate insurance choices and understanding how care expenses interact with income sources like IRAs to minimize taxes. Traditional and hybrid policies offer slightly different tax advantages. Consult your tax advisor to optimize your strategy before care is needed.

When care is needed, tax planning shifts from a long-term strategy to a year-by-year tactical game.

For example, strategically timing income and deductions can maximize tax savings.

Strategic use of tax-free insurance benefits, combined with careful management of other taxable income sources, can help minimize the overall tax burden during a care event.

Estate and Gift Tax Integration

Long-term care planning intersects with estate and gift tax strategies in important ways that require careful coordination:

- **Asset Protection:** Certain long-term care funding approaches provide asset protection benefits that complement estate planning goals. This is particularly valuable in situations such as blended families or when providing for beneficiaries with special needs, where protecting specific assets for designated purposes becomes crucial.

- **Wealth Transfer Timing:** Long-term care insurance helps preserve your assets for eventual transfer to heirs. Meanwhile, certain estate planning techniques can create tax-efficient ways to fund your care needs. This coordination ensures you have resources for both care and legacy goals.

- **Trust Integration:** Proper planning ensures that trust structures don't inadvertently restrict access to funds needed for care while still achieving your estate planning objectives. The right trust language can provide flexibility for changing care needs.

The most effective planning approaches leverage these connections. For example, hybrid long-term care policies can provide tax-qualified long-term care benefits during your lifetime while potentially preserving a death benefit for your heirs if care isn't needed or if benefits aren't fully used.

Separately, traditional life insurance placed within an irrevocable life insurance trust (ILIT) can create tax-free legacy assets outside your taxable estate (when properly structured from the start), while freeing up other assets for potential care needs.

Each approach serves distinct planning objectives and should be evaluated with qualified advisors who understand both long-term care and estate planning.

The ultimate goal is ensuring that the legal structures designed to protect your legacy don't become barriers to accessing the care you need. This requires that your planning documents and funding strategies work together harmoniously, not in opposition.

Tax-Efficient Funding Strategies

Integrating long-term care planning with tax strategy helps identify the most efficient sources for paying premiums or care expenses:

- **HSA Funding:** Health Savings Accounts offer a powerful triple tax advantage for long-term care planning. First, your contributions to an HSA are tax-deductible. Second, any growth in your HSA is tax-free. Third, when you use these funds to pay for eligible long-term care insurance premiums, those withdrawals are completely tax-free.[121] Note that the IRS sets annual age-based limits on how much you can use for these premiums, but this remains one of the most tax-efficient funding methods available.

- **Using an IRA:** You cannot pay long-term care premiums directly from an IRA, but you can use IRA withdrawals to fund coverage. The most common approach is a 10-pay structure, taking systematic withdrawals over a decade to pay premiums on a hybrid long-term care policy. These withdrawals, taxed as ordinary income, fund premiums for an asset-based (hybrid) long-term care policy. This strategy transforms tax-deferred IRA funds into tax-free long-term care benefits and a potential tax-free death benefit. Note that this approach is most appropriate for individuals at least age 59½ to avoid early withdrawal penalties.

- **Tax-Free 1035 Exchanges:** A powerful opportunity exists to convert existing financial products into long-term care protection without triggering taxes, thanks to the Pension Protection Act of 2006. If you own an annuity or life insurance policy with accumulated cash value, you can exchange it for a hybrid long-term care policy through what's called a "1035 exchange." This exchange must happen directly between insurance companies—you can't take possession of the money yourself. What makes this strategy especially valuable is that it allows you to use both your original investment and any growth in your existing policies to pay for future care expenses completely tax-free. It's like transforming assets you already own into a more efficient form of long-term care protection, with significant tax advantages that weren't available before this legislation.

- **Optimizing Withdrawal Sequence:** A coordinated plan dictates the most tax-efficient order for tapping assets to fund premiums or out-of-pocket care costs. While the conventional wisdom often suggests using taxable accounts first, the optimal sequence should be personalized based on your specific situation, tax bracket, and projected future needs. This strategic sequencing helps preserve your tax-advantaged accounts longer, minimizes your overall tax burden, prevents unnecessary jumps into higher tax brackets, and protects your income-generating assets.

These strategies require careful coordination between your tax professional, a certified long-term care specialist and/or your financial advisor. The optimal solution is rarely a single strategy but a custom-built combination designed by a collaborative team.

IMPLEMENTATION AND MONITORING

Creating an integrated plan is only the first step. Effective implementation and ongoing monitoring are what ensure your plan remains a powerful, relevant tool, not an outdated document.

The Blueprint for Implementation

A successful integrated plan is built in a specific sequence to prevent critical gaps:

1. **Synchronize Your Legal Documents:** Your attorney must ensure your powers of attorney, healthcare directives, and trusts are aligned with your care preferences and explicitly grant the authority needed to manage insurance benefits and care decisions.

2. **Execute Your Funding Strategy:** Formally implement the chosen funding approach—whether traditional long-term care insurance, hybrid policies, or self-funding—with the correct account structures and ownership arrangements in place.

3. **Brief Your Inner Circle:** Communicate the relevant details of your plan to the family members or trusted friends who will act as your advocates, decision-makers, or care coordinators.

4. **Establish Your Professional Team:** Solidify the communication protocols among your advisory team to ensure seamless collaboration when future decisions are needed.

5. **Codify Your Care Preferences:** Create and distribute a clear document detailing your personal priorities for care, from location to provider type, to guide your family and advocates.

This sequence is critical. For instance, your attorney needs to know the specifics of your long-term care policy to ensure your Power of Attorney document grants the explicit authority needed to file claims and manage benefits on your behalf. Without this, your plan could be paralyzed when you need it most.

Staying Ahead of Life: When to Review Your Plan

Even the best plans must adapt. Certain life events should trigger an immediate plan reassessment:

- **Health Changes:** A new diagnosis or a shift in your functional ability

- **Family Transitions:** A marriage, divorce, death, or relocation within your core family

- **Financial Shifts:** A significant change in your assets, income, or retirement trajectory

- **Tax Law Changes:** Modifications to rules affecting medical expenses, insurance, or estates

- **Insurance Market Evolution:** The introduction of new products or features that could enhance your plan

While these events are clear triggers, the most resilient plans are reviewed annually. This scheduled check-in with your advisory team ensures your strategy remains aligned with your life and the current legal landscape.

> **BOTTOM LINE:** Your integrated long-term care plan requires ongoing attention and periodic updates to remain effective. Regular reviews ensure it evolves with your changing circumstances and continues protecting what matters most.

⊙ NAVIGATOR STORY

WHEN YOUR SAFETY NET RELOCATES TO SEATTLE

When Margaret and David Reyes, both 78 and living in Florida, met with their advisor for their annual review, they shared exciting news: their only daughter, Christine, who lived just 20 minutes away, had accepted a Chief Operating Officer position in Seattle. The Reyes had always assumed Christine would be their primary support if either needed care.

Their advisor flagged the implications immediately. "Who becomes your local support network now?" he asked. "And what does this mean for your care preferences?"

The question hit hard. Margaret had always pictured recovering from any health event at home, with Christine nearby to coordinate caregivers and handle logistics. That assumption was no longer realistic.

Over the next two months, they made key adjustments: updated healthcare proxies to include a trusted neighbor and longtime friend, revised care preferences to reflect a greater likelihood of needing professional care coordination, and reviewed their existing long-term care coverage to confirm it was adequate given the new reality.

Coincidentally, six months after Christine's move, David suffered a minor stroke. Margaret was overwhelmed—but the plan held. "If we hadn't had that conversation when we did, I would have been paralyzed trying to figure this out alone," Margaret recalls. "Our advisor helped us see what was coming before it arrived."

CREATING A UNIFIED FAMILY WEALTH STRATEGY

Perhaps the most powerful benefit of integrated planning is its ability to transform a financial strategy into a unified approach to your family's wealth and well-being that spans generations.

This approach recognizes that a care event impacts not just one person, but the entire family.

Beyond Financial Integration

True integration extends beyond financial and legal mechanics to include your family's values, communication, and decision-making. This broader approach is designed to:

- **Set Clear Roles and Expectations:** Everyone understands who will fulfill which responsibilities if care is needed, preventing confusion during a crisis.

- **Pre-Empt Family Conflict:** It addresses potential sources of disagreement, like money or caregiving duties, before they can damage relationships.

- **Preserve Family Relationships:** It provides a framework that allows a spouse to remain a spouse and a child to remain a child, rather than defaulting to the stressful dynamic of full-time caregiver.

Experience shows that families who engage in this comprehensive planning report significantly higher satisfaction with care outcomes and experience far less caregiver burnout.

Multi-Generational Planning Opportunities

Integrated extended care planning also creates powerful multi-generational opportunities:

- **Protecting Educational Goals:** Using insurance to handle care costs can protect assets earmarked for a grandchild's education.

- **Ensuring Business Succession:** A solid plan can facilitate a smoother business transition from one generation to the next.

- **Securing Your Legacy:** It ensures that assets intended for philanthropic goals or family inheritance are not liquidated to pay for care.

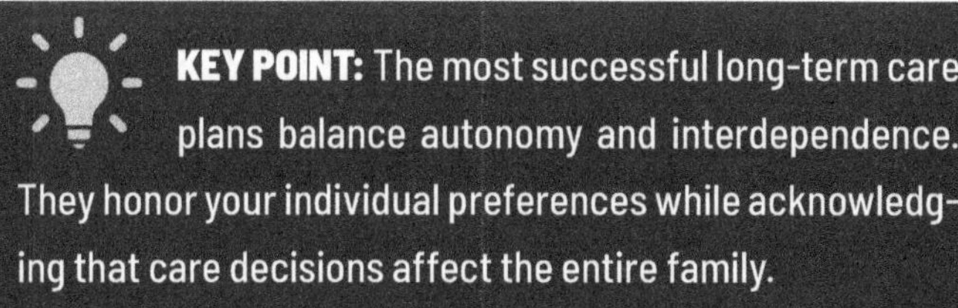

These strategies are most effective when the next generation is included appropriately in the conversation.

While adult children shouldn't drive their parents' decisions, their awareness and input can help create a more resilient and unified family strategy.

 NAVIGATOR STORY

THE FAMILY LEGACY APPROACH

The Russo family transformed their approach to long-term care planning when they shifted from viewing it as an individual concern to seeing it as part of their overall family legacy strategy.

Antonio and Maria Russo, both in their early 70s, had built a successful family restaurant business over four decades. Their initial resistance to long-term care planning stemmed from seeing it as just another insurance expense. During a comprehensive family meeting facilitated by their advisor, their perspective changed dramatically.

"Our advisor showed us how Mom and Dad's potential care needs could derail not just their retirement, but our entire family's financial future," explains their daughter Sofia, who was preparing to take over the business. "We mapped out exactly how unplanned care costs could force a premature sale of the business, deplete the education funds for my children, and eliminate our family's annual contribution to the community food bank my parents helped establish."

Their integrated plan included specific provisions: a combination of traditional long-term care insurance and hybrid solutions for Antonio and Maria that aligned with their family business succession timeline, protected education funding for their three grandchildren, and preserved their philanthropic commitments.

"We stopped seeing Mom and Dad's long-term care insurance as just an expense and started seeing it as protection for everything else we wanted to accomplish as a family," Sofia continues. "That shift in perspective changed our entire approach to family financial decisions. Now we evaluate every major financial move by asking how it affects our collective legacy, not just individual needs."

☑ ACTION STEPS CHECKLIST

All worksheets and templates for this book are online at
WWW.YOURRETIREMENTBLINDSPOT.COM/RESOURCES
Complete them as digital forms or download PDFs. Scan the QR code here:

1. Schedule a coordination meeting with your financial advisor, long-term care specialist, estate planning attorney, and tax professional to review your current planning integration.

2. Create a comprehensive inventory of how your long-term care plan intersects with your retirement strategy, estate plan, and tax approach.

3. Review your legal documents specifically for provisions that address long-term care scenarios and decision-making.

4. Develop a monitoring schedule with specific review triggers based on your personal health, family, and financial circumstances.

5. Initiate appropriate family conversations about how your long-term care plan fits within your broader family wealth and legacy objectives.

TAKING ACTION

Long-term care planning knowledge is only valuable when transformed into concrete action.

Creating a personalized plan requires systematic implementation across multiple dimensions—personal, financial, legal, and interpersonal—to protect both assets and quality of life.

The planning process must be approached methodically, with careful attention to both detail and the bigger picture, resulting not just in documentation but in genuine peace of mind.

This section guides you through creating your plan, working effectively with professionals, navigating essential family conversations, and maintaining your plan as circumstances change.

CREATING YOUR PERSONALIZED LONG-TERM CARE PLAN

- *The 7-step framework for building your personalized plan*

- *Why confronting your personal risk profile is the essential first step*

- *How to align financial strategies with realistic cost projections*

- *The legal documents required to ensure your plan is actionable*

- *Communication strategies to prevent family conflict and confusion*

FROM KNOWLEDGE TO ACTION: THE IMPLEMENTATION IMPERATIVE

Throughout this book, we've explored the many dimensions of long-term care planning. Now, it's time to translate that knowledge into concrete action by creating your personalized plan.

Recent research from Lincoln Financial Group reveals compelling insights about the value of long-term care planning: 94% of Americans surveyed acknowledge that having a long-term care plan would help them feel more confident about their financial future, and an overwhelming 99% believe a long-term care plan would make things easier on their adult children.[122]

These statistics underscore both the personal peace of mind and family protection that proactive planning provides.

BOTTOM LINE: Knowledge is not a plan. This chapter provides the 7-step framework to turn what you've learned into a concrete, personalized strategy tailored to your specific situation, preferences, and values.

THE SEVEN-STEP LONG-TERM CARE PLANNING PROCESS

Creating an effective long-term care plan involves seven interconnected steps, each building on the last to create a comprehensive and resilient strategy:

1. **Confront Your Reality:** Assess your personal risk factors based on health history, genetics, and lifestyle

2. **Clarify Your Care Preferences and Values:** Define what quality of life means to you and your family's role

3. **Assess Your Financial Readiness:** Evaluate your resources and capacity to fund extended care

4. **Design Your Funding Strategy:** Choose the optimal combination of insurance, savings, and other resources

5. **Establish Your Legal Authority:** Ensure proper documentation for decision-making and care coordination

6. **Create Your Family Playbook:** Develop clear communication and implementation guidelines

7. **Keep Your Plan Relevant:** Build in regular review and adjustment processes

With the framework in view, let's begin where every sound plan must: with an honest assessment of your personal reality.

STEP 1: Confront Your Reality: Your Personal Risk Profile

This step clarifies your real-world risk drivers so you can prepare for likely scenarios, not guess at unlikely ones. This isn't about predicting the future, it's about preparing for the possibilities based on the facts at hand.

Your personal risk assessment should include:

- **Family Health History:** This is a critical, non-negotiable part of the assessment. Having a first-degree relative (parent or sibling) with Alzheimer's disease, for example, can increase your own risk significantly.[123]

- **Current Health and Lifestyle:** Document your current health status, medications, and lifestyle factors (like diet and exercise) that influence your long-term health trajectory.

- **Geographic Location:** Care costs vary dramatically by location. Data from industry research, such as the Genworth Cost of Care Survey, reveals that costs can differ by as much as 30% between neighboring counties, making your location a critical factor.[124]

- **Your Home Environment:** Analyze your current housing for its suitability for aging in place. An honest assessment now can reveal whether future modifications could extend your independence.

> **KEY POINT:** Stop trying to predict if you will need care. Instead, use the facts you know today—your family history, health, and lifestyle—to build a plan for how you will handle it. This is the foundation of smart, realistic planning.

STEP 2: Clarify Your Care Preferences and Values

In this step, you translate personal values into care directives that preserve dignity, autonomy, and relationships, reducing confusion and emotional burden later. These preferences become your North Star for every subsequent decision. This isn't a financial exercise; it's a personal one. Consider these core questions:

- **Your Ideal Care Setting:** Where do you want to receive care? While "at home" is the common answer, think through different scenarios. What if you need 24/7 supervision? What if your spouse can no longer manage? Acknowledging these possibilities allows for more realistic planning.

- **Your Family's Role:** This is a crucial, often overlooked conversation. Do you want your children to be hands-on caregivers, or do you prefer they act as care coordinators, managing professionals? Be explicit. This single decision is fundamental to preserving family relationships.

- **Your Core Values:** What matters most to you? Is it maintaining social connections, privacy, spiritual practices, or personal autonomy? These values should be the guiding principles for every decision made on your behalf.

- **Your End-of-Life Wishes:** While distinct from long-term care, your wishes regarding life-sustaining treatment are a critical part of a holistic plan. Ensure your advance directives and living will reflect these preferences clearly.

Ultimately, this step is about codifying what "quality of life" means to you.

For most people, it comes down to three things: preserving dignity, maintaining autonomy, and continuing meaningful relationships.

Documenting your preferences on these matters provides invaluable guidance to your family and ensures your plan truly reflects your wishes. It also reduces the emotional burden on loved ones who might otherwise struggle with difficult decisions during already stressful times.

NAVIGATOR STORY

THE BLUEPRINT

Shayne, a retired engineer, came to his first planning meeting with a detailed spreadsheet. He had compared premium costs, benefit periods, and inflation riders. He was ready to talk numbers. His financial advisor listened patiently, then asked a question that stopped him cold: "Shayne, let's forget the spreadsheet for a moment. If you needed help tomorrow, what does a good day look like for you?"

Shayne was stumped. He had spent weeks analyzing the how of paying for care but had never considered the what—what life would actually be like.

That question changed everything. He and his wife Lily spent the next week talking, not about money, but about what mattered. They agreed that staying in their home was non-negotiable. They wrote down their desire for their children to be advocates, not hands-on caregivers.

Shayne even specified the importance of his morning coffee and reading his latest book on the porch—the small rituals that defined his independence.

When Shayne returned to his financial advisor, his perspective was transformed. "The numbers are just the tools," he said. "That one question helped us design the blueprint first. Now we know exactly what we're building."

STEP 3: Assess Your Financial Readiness

In this step, you measure your actual financial capacity against the hard reality of care costs, identifying gaps before they become crises. This analysis goes beyond a simple net worth statement; it stress-tests your resources against the reality of care costs.

Projecting the Costs: A Sobering Look at the Numbers

Start by estimating potential care costs in your preferred setting. While costs vary by location, recent industry data provides a crucial baseline. The 2025 CareScout survey, for example, found the national median monthly costs to be:[125]

- Non-Medical In-Home Caregiver: $6,673 (based on 44 hours per week for 52 weeks)
- Adult Day Health Care: $2,058 (based on 5 days per week for 52 weeks)
- Assisted Living Community: $6,200 (room and board)
- Nursing Home: $9,581 (semi-private room) to $10,798 (private room)

However, these baseline figures often don't tell the whole story. For instance, memory care is pricier than standard assisted living, typically costing 20-30% more due to specialized staff training and enhanced safety measures for residents with dementia. Please Note: These are just national averages. Costs can swing by thousands of dollars monthly depending on the state you live in.[126]

Furthermore, these costs have consistently outpaced general inflation. Analysis of Bureau of Labor Statistics data reveals that long-term care and adult day services saw inflation of 4.9% between 2023 and 2024, with an average annual increase of 3.7% over the past decade.[127]

This relentless inflation means that a plan based on today's costs will be inadequate tomorrow.

Identifying the Gap: Income vs. Expenses

Extended care exposes the fundamental flaw in most retirement plans: confusing net worth with sustainable income capacity.

Now, compare your sustainable, after-tax retirement income to these potential monthly costs. This is the most critical calculation in your plan.

For many, it reveals a significant funding gap, especially when you factor in the need to preserve enough income for a healthy spouse to maintain their standard of living.

Finally, evaluate the liquidity of your assets. How quickly could you access cash in a crisis without triggering a tax avalanche? When care needs arise, the domino effect of taxes can devastate even well-funded plans.

Forced withdrawals from retirement accounts can push you into higher tax brackets, increase Medicare premiums, and make more of your Social Security benefits taxable—all when you can least afford it.

A plan that looks solid on paper can crumble if funds aren't accessible when needed most.

> **BOTTOM LINE:** Your net worth is not your care fund. The real test is whether your sustainable income can cover years of care costs without sacrificing your spouse's financial security or triggering a cascade of unintended tax consequences.

STEP 4: Design Your Funding Strategy

Your analysis has identified the potential financial gap. Now, you must design a strategy to bridge it. In this step, you architect a customized funding approach by strategically selecting and combining appropriate resources—whether self-funding, insurance solutions, or other options.

This isn't about choosing one single solution; it's about creating a resilient strategy that protects both your care needs and your broader financial objectives.

Consider the primary levers you can pull:

- **Self-Funding:** This is your personal contribution. Determine the portion of care costs you can realistically cover from income and assets without jeopardizing your spouse's lifestyle or your legacy goals. Remember that your capital assets are meant to generate income for your ongoing needs—not to be depleted for care expenses. Even a modest amount of self-funding can be an important part of your overall strategy, but relying exclusively on personal assets creates significant risks: forced liquidation during market downturns, unexpected tax consequences, and potential depletion of resources meant for your spouse or heirs.

- **Insurance Leverage:** This is how you protect your assets from the potential high and unpredictable costs of care. Every person's approach to long-term care planning must be as unique as their individual circumstances. Your specific situation—including health, finances, and personal preferences—will determine which strategies work best for you. Evaluate the role of traditional and hybrid products. The goal of insurance is to transfer the risk, creating a dedicated and leveraged pool of money specifically for care, so your retirement portfolio can remain intact.

- **Government Programs:** Understand your potential eligibility for programs like Veterans benefits or Medicaid. For most people in the planning stage, these are not primary strategies but potential safety nets with significant limitations and strict qualification rules.

- **Home Equity:** For many, home equity is a significant asset. Options like a reverse mortgage can provide liquidity but come with their own set of complex considerations that must be weighed carefully.

The most resilient plans don't rely on a single lever. They create a blended strategy. For example, a plan might use insurance to cover the core costs of care for a defined period, with personal assets designated to cover any additional expenses or to fund the initial elimination period.

The outcome of this step is a clear, written strategy that specifies exactly how potential care costs will be funded, defining the role of each financial resource.

STEP 5: Establish Your Legal Authority

A financial strategy without the right legal documents is like a car without a key—it won't go anywhere when you need it most.

This step ensures that you have a legal framework in place to execute your plan, especially if you become unable to make decisions for yourself.

This legal shield is built on several key components:

- **Durable Powers of Attorney (Financial and Healthcare):** These are the most critical documents for managing your affairs during your lifetime. It's essential to work with an attorney to customize them. Standard, off-the-shelf POA documents often lack the specific powers needed to deal with insurance companies, manage trust assets, or make complex care decisions.

- **Healthcare Directives (Living Will):** This document outlines your wishes for end-of-life medical care, ensuring your preferences are honored.

- **Asset Titling and Beneficiary Designations:** This is a frequently overlooked but critical step. Misaligned titling or outdated beneficiary designations can unintentionally send assets to the wrong person or trigger probate, overriding your entire estate plan.

- **Wills and Trusts:** Ensure your will or trust is up-to-date and works in concert with your long-term care plan, providing for the orderly distribution of assets according to your wishes.

- **Business Succession Documents:** If you own a business, a clear, documented succession plan is non-negotiable to ensure the business can continue to operate smoothly while your personal care needs are met.

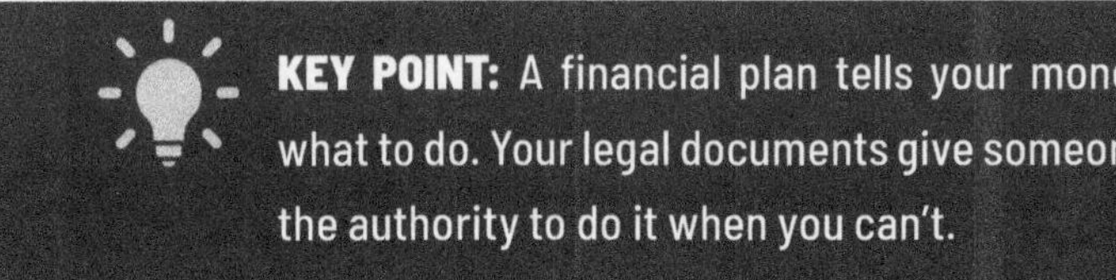

STEP 6: Create Your Family Playbook

When a care crisis hits, communication breakdowns are the primary cause of family conflict and stress.

A well-designed financial and legal plan can be rendered ineffective by family arguments, confusion, and delays.

This step is about creating a clear playbook so that everyone on your team knows their role, what to expect, and how to work together.

Your family playbook should include:

- **The Key Players List:** A comprehensive, up-to-date document with the names and contact information for every person and professional on your team: family members, doctors, attorney, financial advisor, insurance agent, etc. This simple document is invaluable in a crisis.

- **The Information Protocol:** Define who needs to know what. Your financial advisor needs to know when to activate a funding strategy but doesn't need daily health updates. Your healthcare proxy needs all medical details. Clarifying this in advance respects privacy while ensuring the right people have the information they need to act.

- **The Decision-Making Hierarchy:** If you are unable to participate, who is the final decision-maker for healthcare? For finances? If multiple children are involved, is one designated as the lead to prevent stalemates and arguments? This must be clearly documented.

- **The Communication Hub:** How will your family stay informed? A weekly email update from the primary advocate? A private family group chat? Establishing a simple, agreed-upon method prevents the "telephone game" of misinformation and ensures everyone stays on the same page.

STEP 7: Keep Your Plan Relevant: The Review Process

A plan created today is based on today's reality. To remain effective, it must be a living document, adapted to your life as it unfolds.

This final step establishes the process for keeping your plan relevant and powerful year after year.

A formal review process should include:

- **A Scheduled Check-In:** Commit to an annual review with your advisory team. Put it on the calendar like any other critical appointment.

- **Defined Triggers:** Identify life events that will prompt an immediate review outside of the annual schedule. These include major health changes, family transitions (marriage, divorce, death), or significant shifts in your financial situation.

- **A Designated "Quarterback":** Assign one person, often your financial advisor or a trusted family member, the responsibility of initiating and coordinating the review process. Without a designated leader, reviews often fall through the cracks.

- **A System for Documentation:** Create a clear process for documenting any changes to your plan and communicating them to all relevant parties.

KEY POINT: Your long-term care plan is not a static document. It is a dynamic strategy that is only as good as its last review.

This process raises a critical final question: What happens if you can no longer lead these reviews yourself due to cognitive decline?

This is where your entire integrated plan comes together. The legal framework you established in Step 5—specifically your durable power of attorney—is what empowers your designated agent to step in and ensure this review process continues, keeping your plan aligned with your best interests even when you cannot.

 **NAVIGATOR STORY**

THE FAMILY PLAYBOOK

For years, Christopher and Lauren had a folder they called "The 'What If' File." It was a disorganized collection of old will documents, a brochure for a local care facility they'd picked up after helping with Lauren's mother, and a scribbled note with their financial advisor's number. Alongside these were outdated powers of attorney, a faded list of emergency contacts, a printout of their life insurance policy summary, and several handwritten notes about what to do "if something happens."

"It was our financial junk drawer," Christopher says. "It gave us the illusion of being prepared, but in reality, it just created more anxiety. We had pieces, but no plan."

The turning point came when Lauren's mother's Alzheimer's progressed. The family's loving but chaotic response—conflicting calls to doctors, arguments over money, and the sheer exhaustion—was a wakeup call.

"We saw our future, and it was chaos," Lauren admits. "We knew we couldn't do that to our own kids." Working with their advisor, they used the 7-step process to transform their "junk drawer" into a unified "Family Playbook." They had the tough conversations about Lauren's family history. They stress-tested their finances against realistic care costs. They created a funding strategy that blended insurance with a dedicated reserve fund.

The most important step, however, was the family meeting. They sat down with their three adult children, not to burden them, but to walk them through the playbook. They explained the legal documents, the communication plan, and their clear wish for their children to be advocates, not caregivers. "We went from having a folder of anxieties to having a clear, actionable plan," Lauren reflects. "Now, if something happens, our kids don't have to guess. They just have to open the playbook."

OVERCOMING THE ROADBLOCKS

The 7-step process provides the map, but the journey can still have its challenges.

Recognizing these roadblocks as normal parts of the process is the key to moving forward.

- **Procrastination:** The topic can feel overwhelming.

- **Solution:** Break the plan into the small, manageable steps outlined in this chapter. Focus on the empowering aspects of planning, not the fear.

- **Family Disagreement:** Different family members will have different perspectives.

 **Solution:** Start discussions by focusing on shared values, not specific tactics. Consider using a neutral third-party advisor to facilitate difficult conversations.

Information Overload: The complexity of options can be paralyzing.

Solution: Work with a knowledgeable professional who can distill complex information into clear choices. Focus on one decision at a time.

> **BOTTOM LINE:** Planning roadblocks are normal. Acknowledging them is the first step to overcoming them.

YOU DON'T HAVE TO DO THIS ALONE: THE ROLE OF PROFESSIONAL GUIDANCE

While the principles in this book can guide you, the expertise of a professional specializing in extended care planning can be invaluable.

A skilled guide can help you streamline the process, avoid common pitfalls, and provide objectivity during emotional decisions.

When seeking professional guidance, look for a specialist with a proven track record, a fiduciary commitment to your best interests, and a planning philosophy that aligns with your values.

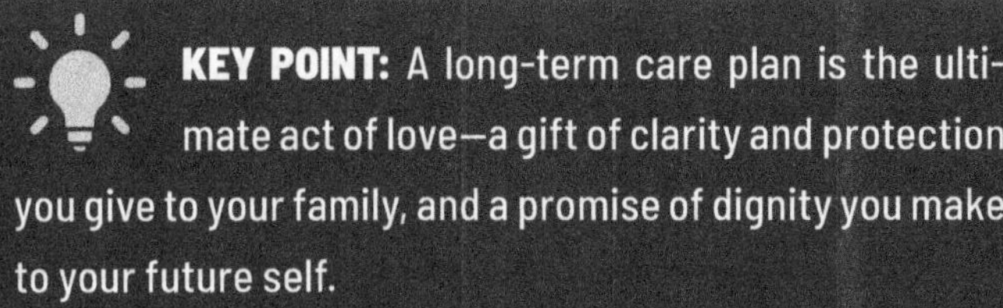

THE ULTIMATE RETURN ON
INVESTMENT: PEACE OF MIND

Ultimately, the true value of this plan isn't measured in dollars or legal clauses.

It's measured in the transformation of anxiety into confidence. It's the profound peace of mind that comes from knowing you have a clear strategy to protect your family, preserve your dignity, and honor your wishes.

While there is no single statistic, countless studies and real-world experience confirm a fundamental truth: families with a clear plan navigate care crises with significantly less stress, conflict, and regret than those who are unprepared.

☑ ACTION STEPS CHECKLIST

All worksheets and templates for this book are online at
WWW.YOURRETIREMENTBLINDSPOT.COM/RESOURCES
Complete them as digital forms or download PDFs. Scan the QR code here: 

1. Schedule a specific time to begin your personal risk assessment, gathering family health history and evaluating your current health status.

2. Use the "Care Preferences Assessment" worksheet discussed in chapter one to outline your care preferences and values, focusing particularly on what matters most to your quality of life.

3. Compile a comprehensive inventory of your financial resources and estimate potential care costs in your preferred setting using the cost-of-care calculator at www.carescout. com/cost-of-care

4. Research long-term care funding options appropriate to your specific situation, considering both insurance and non-insurance approaches.

5. Review your legal documents to ensure they specifically address long-term care scenarios and incapacity management.

WORKING WITH PROFESSIONALS

- Long-term care planning often requires specialized expertise across multiple disciplines

- Core team members typically include financial advisors, certified long-term care specialists, elder law attorneys, and tax professionals

- Finding the right professionals involves research, referrals, credential verification, and thoughtful interviews

- Team structures can be organized as a quarterback model, a collaborative approach, or sequential consultation

- Effective coordination requires clear role definition and communication protocols

- Clients have important responsibilities in the professional relationship

- Family involvement should be carefully structured with clear boundaries

THE VALUE OF PROFESSIONAL GUIDANCE

While the previous chapter outlined a comprehensive framework for creating your long-term care plan, many individuals benefit from professional guidance through this complex process.

Long-term care planning intersects with financial planning, insurance, legal, tax, healthcare, and family systems—making it challenging for any single individual to master all relevant aspects alone.

Professional guidance isn't just about technical expertise; it also provides an objective perspective, accountability, and coordination across these complex domains.

This chapter explores how to identify, evaluate, and work effectively with the various professionals who can support your long-term care planning journey.

BOTTOM LINE: The right professional team transforms a complex, emotional problem into a clear, manageable strategy.

UNDERSTANDING THE LONG-TERM CARE PROFESSIONAL ECOSYSTEM

Long-term care planning intersects with multiple professional disciplines, each bringing specialized expertise to different aspects of your plan.

Understanding the roles and qualifications of these professionals is the first step in assembling an effective team.

Financial Advisors

Financial advisors help integrate long-term care planning with your broader financial strategy. They analyze how potential care needs might impact your retirement security, evaluate funding options, and develop strategies that balance long-term protection with other financial goals.

> **KEY POINT:** A financial advisor's most important role is to ensure that, if long-term care becomes necessary, the strategy to pay for it doesn't undermine the strategy to protect your retirement income or preserve your financial commitments and lifestyle.

Financial advisors operate under different compensation models, including fee-only advisors (compensated solely by client fees with no commissions), fee-based advisors (receiving both client fees and potential product commissions), and commission-based advisors (compensated primarily through product sales commissions). Many advisors are also Registered Investment Advisors (RIAs), which is a regulatory designation requiring fiduciary duty to clients regardless of their compensation model.

Relevant credentials include Certified Financial Planner™ (CFP®), Chartered Financial Consultant® (ChFC®), and Retirement Income Certified Professional® (RICP®). CFP® professionals have fiduciary obligations when providing financial planning services.

When evaluating financial advisors for long-term care planning, look for those who demonstrate a holistic approach rather than product-focused recommendations. The most qualified professionals recognize that extended care planning is an essential part of a comprehensive retirement, tax, and estate strategy—not an afterthought or something to be left entirely to chance.

Long-Term Care Insurance Specialists

These professionals focus specifically on long-term care funding solutions and the complex landscape of long-term care planning.

They provide critical expertise on current product offerings, carrier financial strength ratings, appropriate coverage design, application strategies, underwriting considerations, and claims support when benefits need to be accessed.

Long-term care specialists help clients navigate the various funding options available, including traditional long-term care insurance, hybrid products, and alternative funding strategies. Their specialized knowledge allows them to customize solutions based on your health history, financial situation, and specific care preferences. These insurance specialists may operate in two main capacities:

- **Captive Agents:** Represent a single insurance company and offer only that carrier's products

- **Independent Agents:** Contract with multiple insurance carriers, offering a wide range of product options to find the most suitable coverage for your needs

The most widely recognized credential in this field is the Certified in Long-Term Care (CLTC®) designation, which equips professionals with comprehensive training in long-term care planning, including the emotional, physical, and financial consequences of a long-term care event.

> **KEY POINT:** The most effective long-term care specialists prioritize a client-centered planning approach that begins with understanding your unique situation, values, and goals. Their expertise lies in developing personalized strategies that respect your individual circumstances and family dynamics.

The CLTC® program emphasizes a consultative, client-centered approach rather than a product-driven sales process. CLTC® professionals adhere to a Code of Professional Responsibility and ethical guidelines for the promotion and implementation of long-term care insurance.

Many financial advisors also pursue the CLTC® designation to enhance their expertise in this critical area, allowing them to integrate extended care planning seamlessly with broader financial strategies.

When working with a financial advisor on long-term care planning, those holding both financial planning credentials (such as CFP®) and the CLTC® designation offer a valuable combination of comprehensive financial knowledge and specialized long-term care expertise.

When selecting a long-term care specialist, look for professionals who take time to understand your unique situation and family dynamics, explain options clearly without overwhelming technical jargon, and demonstrate a commitment to ongoing education in this rapidly evolving field.

Elder Law Attorneys

Elder law attorneys specialize in legal issues affecting older adults and those with disabilities.

They create powers of attorney and advance directives that specifically address extended care scenarios, develop estate plans that accommodate care needs, and provide guidance on Medicaid planning and Veterans benefits when appropriate.

Relevant credentials include Certified Elder Law Attorney (CELA), Accreditation with the Department of Veterans Affairs, and membership in the National Academy of Elder Law Attorneys (NAELA).

Because this is a highly specialized field, it's crucial to work with an attorney who focuses on elder law, as they often identify critical issues that a general practice attorney might overlook.

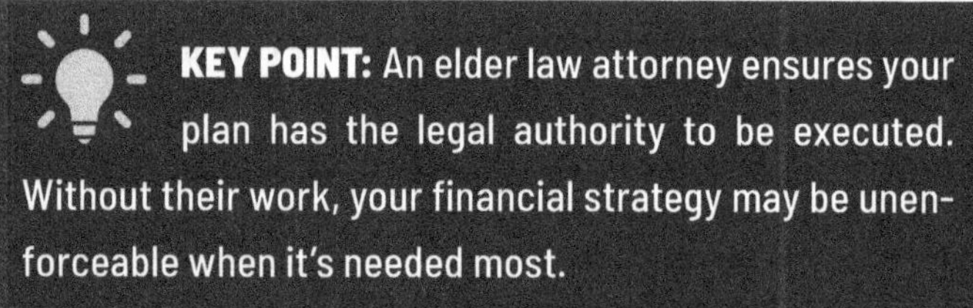

KEY POINT: An elder law attorney ensures your plan has the legal authority to be executed. Without their work, your financial strategy may be unenforceable when it's needed most.

Tax Professionals

Tax professionals help optimize the tax aspects of long-term care planning.

They provide guidance on the tax deductibility of long-term care insurance premiums, the tax treatment of different funding vehicles, the strategic use of medical expense deductions, and the tax implications of various asset transfer strategies.

Types of tax professionals include Certified Public Accountants (CPAs), Enrolled Agents (EAs), and tax attorneys.

The most effective tax professionals for extended care planning understand both the immediate tax implications of planning decisions and the potential long-term tax consequences during care situations.

> **KEY POINT:** A tax professional's role is to prevent unnecessary "leaks" in your financial plan, ensuring that more of your money is available for your care and less is lost to taxes.

NAVIGATOR STORY

CONNECTING THE DOTS

Mark, a 56-year-old business owner, had always managed his own finances. When he started looking into long-term care planning, he approached it the same way: download some forms, read some articles, and find the "best" product.

"I had my business succession plan in one folder and my personal estate plan in another," Mark explains. "It wasn't until I started mapping out what would happen if I actually needed care that I saw the huge, terrifying gap between them. My plans didn't talk to each other."

He realized his standard Power of Attorney wouldn't give his wife the authority to manage business assets, and his personal funds were tied up in ways that made them difficult to access in a crisis. Frustrated, he met with a financial advisor who specialized in long-term care.

"I expected a sales pitch," Mark recalls. "Instead, she said, 'Mark, this isn't an insurance problem; it's a coordination problem.' That one sentence changed everything."

The advisor quarterbacked a team, bringing in Mark's CPA and an elder law attorney. In a single, coordinated meeting, they connected the dots:

- *The attorney drafted a new Power of Attorney with specific provisions for business management.*

- *The CPA identified a tax-efficient way to reposition assets.*

- *The advisor designed a hybrid long-term care plan funded in a way that protected both his family's lifestyle and the company's cash flow.*

"I walked in looking for a product and walked out with a single, integrated strategy," Mark reflects. "My team wasn't just protecting my portfolio; they were protecting my life's work and my family's future. That's a different level of planning."

FINDING AND EVALUATING PROFESSIONALS

Building the right long-term care planning team requires careful research and thoughtful evaluation. Start by identifying potential professionals through a combination of personal referrals, professional associations, and credential verification.

Finding a CLTC (Certified in Long-Term Care) Professional: To locate a CLTC designee, visit the official CLTC website (www. ltc-cltc.com/cltc/findCLTC) which offers a searchable directory of professionals who have completed specialized training in long-term care planning.

These individuals are committed to ethical standards and have demonstrated expertise in helping clients navigate extended care decisions.

Locating Qualified Financial Advisors: In addition to personal referrals, consider using reputable professional association directories. The Financial Planning Association (FPA) (www.plannersearch.org) and the National Association of Personal Financial Advisors (NAPFA) (www.napfa.org) both provide searchable databases of credentialed advisors, many of whom have experience with long-term care and retirement planning.

Look for advisors with designations such as CFP® (Certified Financial Planner) or ChFC® (Chartered Financial Consultant), and ask specifically about their experience with long-term care planning.

Finding Elder Law Attorneys: The National Academy of Elder Law Attorneys (NAELA) (www.naela.org) maintains a directory of attorneys who specialize in elder law, including long-term care, Medicaid planning, and incapacity issues.

Evaluating Professionals: When evaluating potential team members, prioritize those who devote a significant portion of their practice to extended care issues. Specialists are more likely to recognize opportunities and nuances that generalists might overlook.

Ensure their approach and philosophy align with your values, and that their communication style is clear and responsive.

During initial consultations, observe whether the professional listens carefully to your concerns and tailors their advice, rather than offering a generic presentation.

Key Questions to Ask:

- **For financial advisors:** "How do you integrate long-term care planning into a client's overall financial plan?"

- **For insurance specialists:** "What is your process for determining appropriate coverage levels, and how many insurance carriers do you represent?"

- **For elder law attorneys:** "What percentage of your practice focuses on elder law and incapacity planning?"

- **For all professionals:** "Can you provide an example of how you've helped a client with a situation similar to mine?"

> **BOTTOM LINE:** Choosing your professional team is as much about finding the right fit as it is about finding the right credentials. Take the time to research, interview, and select professionals who not only have the necessary expertise but also understand your unique needs and values.

CREATING AN EFFECTIVE PROFESSIONAL TEAM

Once you've identified the right people, creating an effective team requires intentional coordination. There are three common structures:

- **The Quarterback Model:** One professional (often a financial advisor or certified long-term care specialist) serves as the primary coordinator, bringing in other specialists as needed. This model provides clear leadership and a single point of contact for you.

- **The Collaborative Team Model:** Multiple professionals work together as equals, each contributing their specialized expertise. This model provides deep expertise in each area but requires more coordination from you.

- **The Sequential Consultation Model:** You work with different professionals in sequence rather than simultaneously. This can be cost-effective for simpler situations but risks creating a fragmented plan.

Regardless of the structure, success depends on clear role definitions, secure information-sharing protocols, and regular communication among all team members.

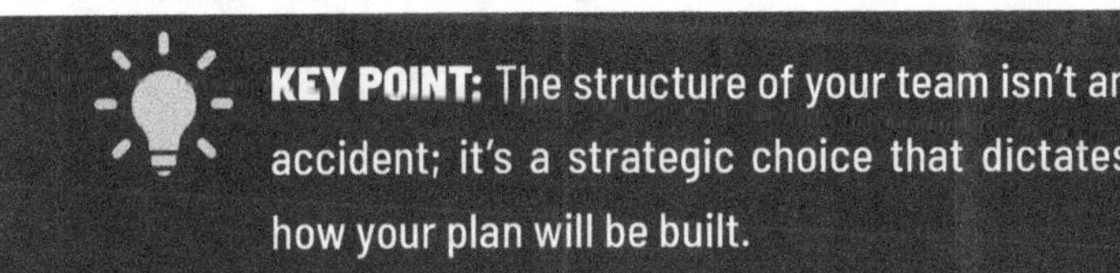

YOUR ROLE ON THE TEAM: HOW TO BE AN EFFECTIVE CLIENT

As the client, you are the most important member of your professional team.

The quality of the plan your team creates is a direct reflection of the quality of the information and engagement you provide.

Your first responsibility is to be clear and candid.

Your team can only build a plan around the priorities you share, so being open about your values, financial constraints, and specific preferences for care is the foundation of a successful strategy.

The more your team knows about what truly matters to you, the better they can tailor a plan that fits your life. Equally important is your role as an active participant.

This is your plan, not your advisor's. This means coming to meetings prepared with questions, reviewing documents thoroughly, and speaking up if you disagree or are confused.

Your active engagement ensures the final plan is one you truly understand and support, transforming it from a binder on a shelf into a strategy you believe in.

Finally, an effective client understands that planning is about managing probabilities, not predicting the future.

Professional guidance provides clarity and strategy, but it cannot eliminate all uncertainty. The best plans are designed to be flexible and evolve over time, adapting to life's inevitable changes.

BOTTOM LINE: You are the CEO of your long-term care plan; your professional team works for you.

 **NAVIGATOR STORY**

THE ROI OF CERTAINTY

As a management consultant, Madison's career was built on one principle: Efficiency. So, when she began her long-term care planning at age 54, she naturally saw professional fees as an inefficiency to be minimized. She spent weeks trying to compare insurance policies online and decipher legal documents.

"I was logging billable hours on my own life, with no clear outcome," she admits. *"I'm an expert in business strategy, not the nuances of long-term care insurance. It was a terrible use of my time."*

Frustrated, she brought the problem to her trusted financial advisor, Liz. "I expected her to just run some numbers," Madison recalls. "Instead, Liz said, 'Madison, my job is to protect your overall financial strategy. For this specific risk, we need a specialist. Let's bring in an expert I partner with.'"

Liz introduced her to a certified long-term care specialist named Roy who didn't just present products; he analyzed Madison's specific health profile and family history to design a funding strategy.

Working together, Liz ensured the plan's funding aligned with Madison's investment goals, while the certified long-term care specialist Roy handled the technical design and underwriting strategy. "The real value was in the coordination," Madison reflects.

"My financial advisor quarterbacked the process, ensuring the insurance piece didn't disrupt my retirement plan. The certified long-term care specialist saved me from making costly mistakes I didn't even know I could make. I didn't just pay for a plan; I invested in certainty and efficiency. For a consultant, that's the best ROI there is."

NAVIGATING FAMILY INVOLVEMENT

Extended care planning often involves family members, creating both opportunities and challenges.

When structured appropriately, family participation can enhance understanding and reduce future conflicts. However, without clear boundaries, it can complicate the process.

Consider including adult children or other trusted family members in initial planning meetings to create a shared understanding of your wishes.

It is crucial, however, to establish clear boundaries regarding decision-making authority. This ensures family members understand their role is to support your plan, not to override it (unless you explicitly grant them that authority).

A skilled advisor can act as a neutral guide during these conversations, helping to focus discussions on shared goals rather than past conflicts. Using tools like a secure digital vault can also simplify sharing documents and ensure everyone has the right information at the right time.

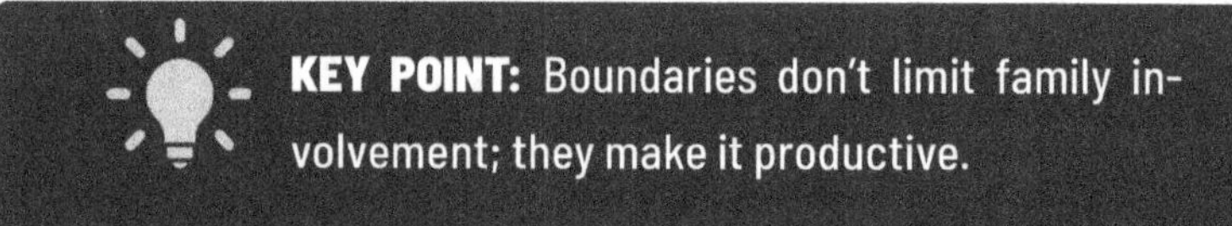

FINDING YOUR BALANCE

The right balance between self-direction and professional support is unique to you. If your financial life is complex, or if family dynamics are challenging, leaning more heavily on a professional team can provide crucial structure and objectivity.

A desire for a third-party perspective or concerns about future health can also point toward greater professional involvement.

Conversely, if your finances are straightforward and your family is aligned on expectations, you may be comfortable taking a more hands-on role, using professionals for specific tasks rather than comprehensive management. There is no single right answer, only the answer that is right for you.

FROM ANXIETY TO ACTION

Ultimately, building your professional team is the critical step that transforms planning from a source of anxiety into a source of confidence.

It's the moment you stop trying to solve a complex, multi-faceted problem on your own and instead assemble the expertise needed to create a real solution.

The most effective professional relationships are true partnerships—combining your personal knowledge and values with professional expertise and guidance.

BOTTOM LINE: A well-chosen professional team doesn't just give you a plan; it gives you the confidence to live your life knowing you're prepared for whatever comes next.

☑ ACTION STEPS CHECKLIST

All worksheets and templates for this book are online at
WWW.YOURRETIREMENTBLINDSPOT.COM/RESOURCES
Complete them as digital forms or download PDFs. Scan the QR code here:

1. Create a list of the specific professional expertise you need based on your unique circumstances and concerns.

2. Research potential professionals using referrals, professional associations, and credential verification.

3. Prepare specific questions for professional interviews that address expertise, approach, and coordination capabilities.

4. Determine which team structure (quarterback, collaborative, or sequential) best fits your preferences and needs.

5. Establish clear processes for information sharing, communication, and regular review among your professional team members.

FAMILY CONVERSATIONS AND MAINTAINING YOUR PLAN

- *Effective family communication is essential for successful long-term care plan implementation*

- *Structured conversations reduce misunderstandings and prevent future conflicts*

- *Timing, participants, setting, and approach significantly impact conversation effectiveness*

- *Common challenges include resistance, family dynamics, and emotional reactions*

- *Regular plan maintenance ensures relevance as circumstances change*

- *Specific triggers should prompt immediate plan reviews*

- *Digital tools can enhance family communication and plan maintenance*

- *Professional support may be valuable for complex family situations*

THE CRITICAL ROLE OF FAMILY COMMUNICATION

Even the most carefully designed long-term care plan may fail without effective family communication.

While previous chapters have addressed the technical aspects of planning, from funding strategies to legal frameworks, this chapter focuses on the human elements that ultimately determine whether your plan will be successfully implemented when needed.

Family conversations about extended care are often avoided due to discomfort with the subject, fear of conflict, or simple procrastination.

However, these conversations are essential for creating shared understanding, establishing clear expectations, and preventing future misunderstandings during an already stressful time.

BOTTOM LINE: A plan without communication is just a secret, and a secret plan is useless in a crisis.

ORCHESTRATING AN EFFECTIVE FAMILY CONVERSATION

Effective family conversations about extended care don't happen by accident—they require thoughtful preparation and structure. The timing of these conversations is critical.

Experience shows that it's far more effective to initiate these discussions during periods of relative calm rather than in the middle of a health crisis.

While there is no "perfect" time, natural openings can present themselves. This might be a scheduled family meeting, a quiet moment during a holiday gathering, or a discussion prompted by the experience of a friend or a relevant news story.

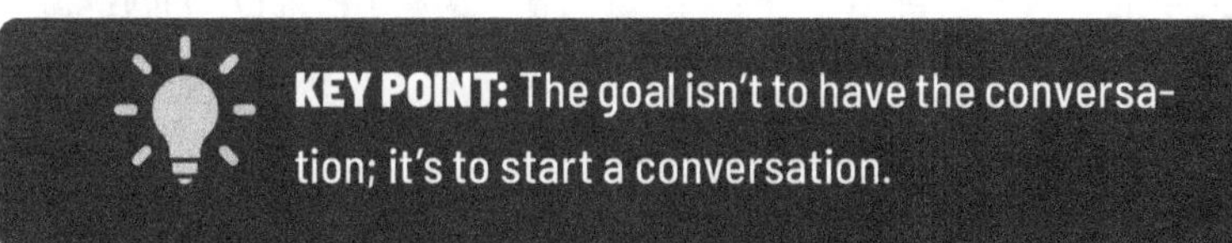

Deciding who should participate requires balancing inclusivity with practicality. It's important to include those who would likely be involved in your care or who have a strong emotional investment in the outcome.

However, remember that different conversations may require different participants. Some discussions are best suited for the entire family, while others are more productive in smaller groups or one-on-one.

The setting and your approach will significantly impact the conversation's tone. Choose a comfortable, private setting with minimal distractions. It's often more effective to frame the conversation as planning for independence and autonomy rather than focusing on potential decline.

Start by sharing your motivations—your desire to protect the family—before diving into specific financial or legal details.

Using structured tools like The Conversation Project (a guide for discussing care preferences) or Five Wishes (an advance directive document) can also provide a helpful framework that keeps the discussion focused and productive.

NAVIGATOR STORY

OLIVIA'S "WHY"

Olivia, a 64-year-old retired teacher, had a comprehensive long-term care plan neatly filed in her desk drawer. But to her two adult children, it was a complete secret.

The silence was broken after a close friend's husband had a sudden stroke, leaving the family to make agonizing decisions in a fog of grief and confusion. "I watched them struggle with guesswork," Olivia says. "I swore I would never put my own children through that."

She scheduled a specific meeting, not a casual chat. When her son and daughter arrived, she began with a simple statement: "I'm not calling this meeting because I'm sick. I'm calling it because I love you both too much to ever make you guess."

She explained her desire to remain at home and outlined the hybrid long-term care policy she had put in place to fund it. Immediately, a debate started. Her son, Jack, argued for the "safety" of a continuing care community, while her daughter, Grace, worried about the logistics of managing home care.

Olivia let them talk, then gently refocused the conversation. "She explained that her plan wasn't just about where she would live, but how," Grace recalls. "She talked about her garden, her church group, and her independence. The insurance wasn't just a policy; it was the tool that made her vision for her own life possible."

That was the turning point. "The moment they understood my 'why,' the arguments stopped," Olivia reflects. "We weren't debating logistics anymore; we were working together to honor my life."

NAVIGATING COMMON COMMUNICATION CHALLENGES

Even with careful preparation, family conversations about extended care planning often encounter challenges. Understanding these common obstacles and having strategies to address them can help maintain productive dialogue.

Many family members initially resist these discussions. This resistance may manifest as changing the subject, making jokes to deflect from a serious topic, expressing excessive optimism that planning isn't necessary, or simply refusing to participate. To address this, it's helpful to acknowledge the discomfort directly but gently.

Experience shows that normalizing this discomfort with statements like, "I know this can be difficult to talk about," can reduce defensive responses. Consider sharing articles or stories that illustrate the benefits of planning—resources like this book offer practical strategies for these exact situations—and be willing to start with less threatening topics before addressing more sensitive issues.

While persistence is important, forcing a conversation can be counterproductive. If resistance continues, try saying something like, "Let's table this for now and talk again in two weeks." This gives everyone time to think without letting the topic disappear entirely.

Extended care planning conversations can also activate existing family dynamics, including sibling rivalries or unresolved conflicts. When these dynamics emerge, it's crucial to focus on shared goals rather than past grievances.

Using "we" language emphasizes a common purpose and helps establish ground rules for respectful communication.

In these situations, a neutral third party—such as a financial advisor, a certified long-term care specialist, or a family therapist—can be invaluable in facilitating a difficult conversation.

Finally, these discussions often evoke strong emotions, including grief about potential decline, anxiety about future responsibilities, or fear about financial security. These feelings can overwhelm rational discussion if not acknowledged.

It's important to create space for emotional expression while maintaining focus on the planning objectives. Experts in family communication agree that conversations that acknowledge and normalize emotional responses are far more likely to result in concrete planning outcomes compared to those that attempt to suppress emotional content.

BOTTOM LINE: Communication challenges aren't a sign of failure; they're a sign you're finally having the right conversation.

MAINTAINING YOUR LONG-TERM CARE PLAN

Long-term care planning is not a one-time event but an ongoing process that requires regular review and adjustment as circumstances change. Without systematic maintenance, even the most carefully designed plan may become outdated or ineffective when needed.

Scheduled Reviews

The most effective approach is to establish a specific schedule for reviewing your plan. Annual reviews are recommended for most situations. During these reviews, assess whether your care preferences have changed, evaluate if your financial strategy remains appropriate, verify that legal documents reflect your current wishes, and confirm that your communication plans still include the right people.

Creating a simple "review checklist" can ensure all aspects of your plan receive attention.

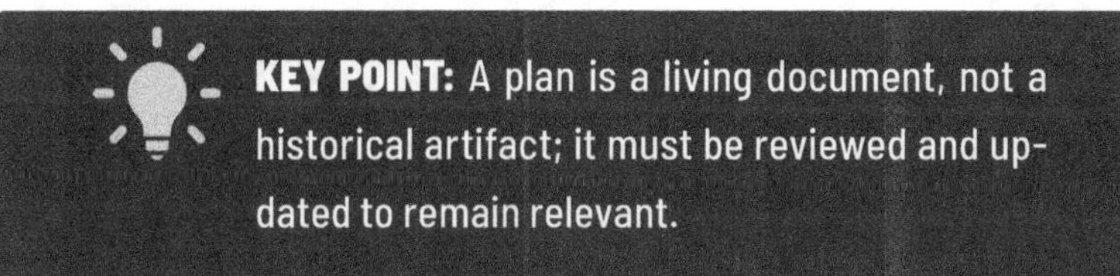

Life Event Triggers

Beyond scheduled reviews, certain life events should prompt an immediate plan reassessment. Personal triggers include significant changes in your health status, new diagnoses, or shifts in your family structure like marriages, divorces, or deaths. Major financial changes, such as an inheritance or business sale, or geographic relocation should also trigger a review.

External triggers include revisions to tax laws that might affect your financial strategies, innovations in insurance products that offer new opportunities, or significant changes to Medicare or Medicaid policy.

Financial planning professionals find that a significant majority of extended care plans require modification following major life events, yet many individuals overlook the need for timely review. Creating a specific list of these triggers increases the likelihood that your plan will be updated when it matters most.

Organizational Tools

Technology can help maintain your plan effectively. Secure digital document storage provides safe access for important papers, with controlled sharing for family members and advisors. Care coordination platforms help families communicate updates and manage responsibilities. Calendar systems can remind you of review dates and important deadlines.

However, these organizational tools work best when they support—rather than replace—regular family conversations and professional guidance. The most effective maintenance approach keeps meaningful human connection at the center of your planning process.

NAVIGATOR STORY

DYLAN'S "DAD CARE PLAYBOOK"

Dylan, a widowed 68-year-old retired engineer, believed that "a plan you don't maintain is a plan that's already failed." He applied this thinking to his long-term care plan with two simple but powerful habits.

First, he created a "Dad Care Playbook"—a secure digital vault containing everything from his will and insurance policies to a simple document outlining his care preferences.

Second, he scheduled an annual "Plan Review" with his two adult children every May right after tax season. "For three years, the meetings were pretty boring," Dylan admits. "We'd just confirm everything was the same and then go to lunch. It felt a little like overkill."

Then, life happened. His daughter, who lived ten minutes away and was his designated healthcare agent, received a major job promotion and moved to another state. "In the past, that news would have sent me into a panic," Dylan says. "But because we had our system, it was just an agenda item for our next meeting."

At their next review, they updated the Playbook, designating his son as the primary healthcare agent and establishing a relationship with a geriatric care manager in Dylan's area who could provide local support if needed. They also added his daughter's neighbor, a retired nurse, as an emergency contact.

"What could have been a crisis became a simple update to our plan," Dylan explains. "My daughter didn't have to feel guilty about her move, and my son didn't have to worry about suddenly taking on responsibilities he wasn't prepared for. The Playbook doesn't just organize my care preferences—it gives my children confidence that we can handle whatever comes next."

WHEN TO BRING IN A PROFESSIONAL

While many families can navigate these conversations on their own, professional guidance can be invaluable, especially if your family has a history of difficult communication, complex dynamics like blended families, or significant disagreements about care.

In these situations, a neutral third party can be the catalyst for a productive discussion.

An elder care manager or a family therapist with expertise in aging can help navigate the emotional currents and keep the conversation focused. A financial advisor or a certified long-term care specialist can ground the discussion in practical reality, connecting family values to concrete funding strategies and care options.

Their role is not to make decisions for you, but to create a structured, safe environment where your family can make decisions together.

THE PROMISE OF A PLAN

This book was never just about insurance policies or legal documents. It was about love, responsibility, and the promises we make—spoken and unspoken—to the people who matter most. It was about transforming the anxiety of "what if" into the confidence of "I'm ready."

Extended care planning is not about preparing for an end; it is about designing how you intend to live the rest of your life, on your own terms. It is the ultimate act of personal responsibility and the ultimate expression of love for your family. It replaces the potential for chaos and guesswork with a clear path forward, guided by your values. Every day you wait, the cost of inaction grows. But today, you have the power to change the future for yourself and for everyone you love.

So, what is the first step? It is not to call an advisor or buy a product. It is simply to decide...

- that you will not leave this to chance.

- that you will not burden your family with agonizing choices during a crisis.

- that your legacy will be one of foresight and protection.

Your journey begins not with a complex financial model, but with a single, courageous conversation. First with yourself, and then with those you love.

The greatest gift you can give your family is a plan and the greatest peace of mind you can give yourself is knowing that a plan is in place.

☑ ACTION STEPS CHECKLIST

All worksheets and templates for this book are online at
WWW.YOURRETIREMENTBLINDSPOT.COM/RESOURCES
Complete them as digital forms or download PDFs. Scan the QR code here:

1. Schedule an initial family conversation about your long-term care preferences and planning approach, considering timing, participants, setting, and structure

2. Create a digital or physical system for organizing and sharing important documents related to your long-term care plan

3. Establish a specific schedule for regular plan reviews, including quarterly, annual, and biennial checkpoints for different plan elements

4. Develop a list of specific events that should trigger immediate plan reviews and share this list with family members and advisors

5. Consider which digital tools might enhance your plan maintenance and family communication, evaluating options for secure document storage, care coordination, and health information management

YOUR LONG-TERM CARE PLANNING JOURNEY BEGINS TODAY

Throughout this book, you've met couples like Liam and Leila, Jeremy and Julie, and countless others who transformed uncertainty into confidence through thoughtful long-term care planning. Their stories share a common thread: they took action before a crisis forced their hand.

You've also witnessed the stark contrast. Couples like Gabriel and Camilla, who faced devastating financial and emotional consequences when long-term care needs arose without warning. The Cohens, whose lack of planning tore their family apart during what should have been a time of coming together. These stories remind us that inaction is also a choice—one with profound consequences.

Long-term care planning isn't about predicting the future. It's about protecting what matters most. Your independence. Your family's wellbeing. Your life's work. The values that define who you are.

Every day you delay is a day of lost opportunity. Insurance becomes more expensive. Health changes limit options. Family dynamics grow more complex.

But today, right now, you have the power to change your family's future.

Here's your next step:

Choose one action from below and complete it within 48 hours:

- Have the conversation with your spouse about care preferences
- Contact a certified long-term care (CLTC®) specialist for a consultation
- Schedule a meeting with your financial advisor to discuss long-term care planning
- Review your current financial plan with long-term care in mind
- Share this book with someone you love

The families who fare best aren't those who never face challenges.

They're those who planned ahead. They're the ones who sleep soundly knowing their wishes will be honored and their loved ones protected.

Your legacy isn't just what you leave behind. It's the burden you choose not to place on those you love.

Begin today. Your future self—and your family—will thank you.

God bless,

Zach Ott

TOOLS & RESOURCES

This section provides access to worksheets, comparison tools, and checklists to help turn planning into action.

APPENDICES

APPENDIX A: LONG-TERM CARE PLANNING WORKSHEETS

All long-term care planning worksheets can be found at **www.yourretirementblindspot.com/resources**

APPENDIX B: GLOSSARY OF TERMS

- **Advance Directive:** A legal document stating your medical preferences if you cannot speak for yourself, including guidance on life-sustaining treatments and comfort care.

- **Activities of Daily Living (ADLs):** Bathing, dressing, eating, transferring, toileting, and continence; inability to perform two or more, or severe cognitive impairment, typically triggers long-term care benefit eligibility under tax-qualified rules.

- **Adult Day Care:** Supervised daytime programs that provide social, health, and supportive services in a group setting; participants return home in the evening.

- **Aging in Place:** Living safely, independently, and comfortably at home and in the community as needs change.

- **Assisted Living Facility (ALF):** Residential setting offering housing, personal assistance with daily activities, medication support, and some health services, without 24/7 skilled nursing.

- **Bed Reservation Benefit:** A policy feature that pays to hold a facility bed during a temporary hospital stay, subject to the policy's limits.

- **Benefit Period:** The length of time benefits are available once eligible (e.g., two, three, or five years), often derived from a pool-of-money calculation.

- **Benefit Triggers:** Conditions that qualify an insured for benefits, typically the need for substantial assistance with at least two ADLs for at least 90 days, or severe cognitive impairment requiring substantial supervision, as certified by a Licensed Health Care Practitioner.

- **Calendar-Day vs. Service-Day Elimination Period:** Calendar-day counts every day after eligibility begins; service-day counts only days when covered services are received.

- **Care Coordination:** Professional guidance to organize services, providers, and a Plan of Care; may be built into the policy or provided by a Care Manager.

- **Care Manager:** A professional, typically a nurse or social worker, who assesses needs, develops a Plan of Care, coordinates services, and monitors outcomes.

- **Cash Indemnity (Per Diem):** A benefit model that pays a fixed amount when eligible, regardless of actual expenses, up to policy or tax limits.

- **Chronic Illness (Tax-Qualified):** Status certified by a Licensed Health Care Practitioner indicating the individual needs substantial assistance with at least two ADLs for at least 90 days, or has a severe cognitive impairment requiring substantial supervision.

- **Cognitive Impairment:** A decline in memory, orientation, judgment, or reasoning that requires supervision for safety.

- **Coinsurance:** A cost-sharing percentage paid by the insured on covered expenses; uncommon in modern individual LTC policies.

- **Community-Based Services:** Programs that help people remain at home, such as adult day health care, respite care, transportation, and meal services.

- **Continuing Care Retirement Community (CCRC):** A multi-level community providing independent living, assisted living, and skilled nursing on one campus, allowing residents to remain as needs progress.

- **Coordination of Benefits:** Rules that prevent duplicate payments when multiple coverages apply (e.g., Medicare, workers' compensation); some policies count Medicare-paid days toward the Elimination Period if eligibility criteria are met.

- **Custodial Care:** Non-medical assistance with ADLs and supervision for cognitive impairment that does not require skilled providers.

- **Daily/Monthly Benefit:** The maximum the policy pays per day or per month for eligible services; monthly buckets can reduce day-to-day benefit "waste."

- **Durable Power of Attorney (Financial):** A legal document authorizing an agent to act on your behalf in financial and legal matters if incapacitated.

- **Elimination Period (EP):** A waiting period (a deductible measured in time) after benefit eligibility before the insurer begins paying benefits.

- **Grace Period:** The time after a premium due date during which payment can be made to keep the policy in force.

- **Guaranteed Renewable:** A contractual guarantee that the insurer cannot cancel coverage if premiums are paid; premiums may change by class, not individually.

- **Health Insurance Portability and Accountability Act (HIPAA) / IRC §7702B:** Federal standards for tax-qualified long-term care insurance, including benefit triggers, Plan of Care requirements, and tax treatment of premiums and benefits.

- **Healthcare Power of Attorney:** A legal document designating an agent to make healthcare decisions if you cannot.

- **Home Care:** Care delivered in the home, including personal care, homemaker services, and some skilled services, as outlined in the Plan of Care.

- **Home Health Aide:** A trained caregiver who assists with ADLs, supervision, and routine health tasks in the home setting.

- **Home Modification:** Changes to a residence to improve safety and accessibility (e.g., ramps, grab bars, stair lifts); sometimes covered by policies with stated limits.

- **Hospice Care:** Comfort-focused care for serious illness, generally when life expectancy is limited; emphasizes symptom relief and quality of life.

- **Hybrid (Asset-Based) Long-Term Care Insurance:** A life insurance or annuity policy that includes long-term care benefits. If care is needed, the policy pays LTC benefits (often through an acceleration and/or extension rider); if not, it pays a death benefit (life chassis) or maintains annuity value (annuity chassis). Funding often uses single-premium or limited-pay designs, with potential guarantees, cash value, or Return of Premium features. Benefits may be Reimbursement or Cash Indemnity; verify tax-qualified status under IRC §7702B versus chronic/accelerated illness riders under §101(g).

- **Informal Caregiver:** An unpaid caregiver, such as a spouse, family member, or friend, who assists with ADLs, IADLs, and supervision.

- **Inflation Protection:** A feature that increases policy benefits over time, commonly 3% or 5% compound, to help maintain purchasing power.

- **Instrumental Activities of Daily Living (IADLs):** Tasks that support independent living, including meal preparation, housekeeping, managing money, transportation, shopping, and communication.

- **Licensed Health Care Practitioner (LHP):** A qualified professional (e.g., physician, registered nurse) who can certify chronic illness and author or update the Plan of Care.

- **Long-Term Care Insurance:** Insurance that helps pay for long-term care services at home, in community settings, assisted living, or skilled nursing facilities.

- **Medicaid:** A joint federal–state program that may cover long-term care for people who meet income and asset requirements; eligibility often requires spend down and may involve estate recovery.

- **Medicare:** Federal health insurance primarily for people age 65 and older; covers limited skilled care under specific conditions and does not cover custodial long-term care.

- **Memory Care:** Specialized, secure care for people with Alzheimer's disease or other dementias, often within assisted living or nursing facilities.

- **Nursing Home:** A facility providing 24-hour skilled nursing and rehabilitation services.

- **Palliative Care:** Specialized medical care focused on relief from symptoms and stress of serious illness, at any stage, alongside curative treatment when applicable.

- **Partnership Policy (Long-Term Care Partnership):** A tax-qualified long-term care policy that meets state Partnership standards and can provide dollar-for-dollar asset disregard for Medicaid eligibility after policy benefits are exhausted. Requirements and availability vary by state.

- **Pension Protection Act (PPA) of 2006:** Federal law allowing favorable tax treatment for certain long-term care benefits and enabling qualified LTC benefits from specific annuity or life insurance contracts.

- **Personal Care:** Hands-on assistance with ADLs, including bathing, dressing, and grooming.

- **Plan of Care (POC):** A written plan, prepared by a Licensed Health Care Practitioner, detailing the covered services, providers, and frequency of care; updated as needs change.

- **Pool of Money:** The total maximum dollar amount available, commonly calculated as Benefit Amount × Benefit Period; unused monthly benefits remain available for future use.

- **Pre-Existing Condition:** A prior health condition relevant to underwriting; some group policies may include a temporary post-issue exclusion period, while most individual policies do not.

- **Reimbursement Model:** A benefit model that pays actual covered expenses up to the policy maximum for eligible services and providers.

- **Respite Care:** Short-term relief for primary caregivers through temporary care provided to the insured.

- **Restoration of Benefits:** A feature that reinstates used benefits after a specified recovery period without claims, subject to policy terms.

- **Shared Care:** A feature allowing spouses or partners to access each other's benefits or a third shared pool, according to policy rules.

- **Skilled Care:** Care provided by, or under the supervision of, licensed health professionals, such as registered nurses or therapists.

- **Spend Down:** Reducing countable assets to meet Medicaid financial eligibility limits for long-term care services.

- **Step-Down Limitations (Legacy Policies):** Outdated provisions, common in older contracts, that required prior hospitalization or facility stays before home care benefits; not permitted in modern tax-qualified policies.

- **Traditional Long-Term Care Insurance:** A standalone policy designed specifically for LTC, typically with periodic premiums and no death benefit component.

- **Unintentional Lapse/Reinstatement:** A right to reinstate a lapsed policy within a defined period if lapse occurred due to cognitive impairment or loss of functional capacity, subject to policy terms and proof.

- **Waiver of Premium:** A feature that suspends premium payments while covered benefits are being received, as defined by the policy.

COMPLIANCE NOTE: HIPAA (IRC §7702B) defines standards for tax-qualified LTC insurance, including benefit triggers, Plan of Care requirements, and tax treatment. IRC §101(g) governs certain accelerated/chronic illness riders. NAIC model regulations guide consumer protections, definitions, and policy standards. Consult state-specific statutes and the policy for controlling definitions.

ONE-LINE DISCLAIMER: This glossary is for educational purposes only and does not modify, replace, or interpret any insurance contract or legal document; refer to your actual policy and applicable law for controlling terms.

APPENDIX C: RESOURCE DIRECTORY

Government Resources

Medicare

Website: www.medicare.gov

Phone: 1-800-MEDICARE (1-800-633-4227)

Description: Official U.S. government site for Medicare information, including coverage details, enrollment, and finding healthcare providers.

Medicaid

Website: www.medicaid.gov

Description: Federal site with information about Medicaid programs, eligibility, and links to state Medicaid agencies.

Administration for Community Living

Website: www.acl.gov

Phone: 202-401-4634

Description: Federal agency that works to maximize the independence, well-being, and health of older adults, people with disabilities, and their families and caregivers.

Eldercare Locator

Website: eldercare.acl.gov

Phone: 1-800-677-1116

Description: A public service of the U.S. Administration on Aging that connects older Americans and their caregivers with local support resources.

National Institute on Aging

Website: www.nia.nih.gov

Phone: 1-800-222-2225

Description: Leads a broad scientific effort to understand the nature of aging and extend healthy active years of life.

Veterans Affairs (VA) Benefits

Website: www.caregiver.va.gov

Phone: 1-800-827-1000

Description: Information about VA long-term care services and support for eligible veterans.

The Aid & Attendance Benefit

Website: americanveteransaid.com/aid-attendance-benefit/

Description: Special benefit to war era veterans and their surviving spouses called Aid and Attendance. This is a tax-free benefit designed to provide financial assistance to help cover the cost of long-term care in the home, in an assisted living facility, or in a nursing home.

Social Security Administration

Website: www.ssa.gov

Phone: 1-800-772-1213

Description: Information about Social Security retirement, disability, and survivors' benefits.

Non-Profit Organizations

AARP

Website: www.aarp.org

Phone: 1-888-687-2277

Description: Nonprofit organization that empowers people to choose how they live as they age, with extensive resources on caregiving and long-term care.

Alzheimer's Association

Website: www.alz.org

Phone: 1-800-272-3900

Description: Leading voluntary health organization in Alzheimer's care, support, and research.

Family Caregiver Alliance

Website: www.caregiver.org

Phone: 1-800-445-8106

Description: Provides information, education, services, research, and advocacy for family caregivers.

National Council on Aging

Website: www.ncoa.org

Phone: 571-527-3900

Description: Nonprofit service and advocacy organization representing older adults and the community organizations that serve them.

National Alliance for Caregiving

Website: www.caregiving.org

Description: Coalition of national organizations focused on advancing family caregiving through research, innovation, and advocacy.

The SCAN Foundation

Website: www.thescanfoundation.org

Description: Charity dedicated to creating a society where older adults can access health and supportive services to age with dignity, independence, and choice.

National Adult Day Services Association

Website: www.nadsa.org

Phone: 1-877-745-1440

Description: The leading voice of the adult day service community, providing advocacy, education, and resources.

Professional Associations

National Academy of Elder Law Attorneys (NAELA)

Website: www.naela.org

Phone: 703-942-5711

Description: Association of attorneys who specialize in legal issues affecting older adults and people with disabilities.

American Association of Daily Money Managers

Website: www.aadmm.com

Phone: 877-326-5991

Description: Organization for professionals who assist older adults and others with routine financial matters.

Aging Life Care Association

Website: www.aginglifecare.org

Phone: 520-881-8008

Description: Association of professional care managers who help families care for older relatives.

National Alliance for Care at Home

Website: www.allianceforcareathome.org

Description: The largest organization representing, advocating for, educating, and connecting providers of care in the home for millions across the US who depend on that care.

American Health Care Association

Website: www.ahcancal.org

Phone: 202-842-4444

Description: Federation of affiliated state health organizations representing long-term and post-acute care providers.

Financial Planning Association

Website: www.onefpa.org

Phone: 800-322-4237

Description: Professional organization for certified financial planners and those who support the financial planning process.

Online Tools and Calculators

Genworth Cost of Care Survey

Website: www.genworth.com/aging-and-you/finances/cost-of-care.html

Description: Annual study of long-term care costs across the United States, with cost projections and comparison tools.

The Federal Long Term Care Insurance Program

Website: www.ltcfeds.gov/tools/cost-of-care

Description: Tool to estimate potential long-term care costs based on location and care preferences.

Medicare Nursing Home Compare
Website: www.medicare.gov/care-compare/
Description: Official tool for comparing nursing homes certified by Medicare and Medicaid.

Benefits Checkup
Website: www.benefitscheckup.org
Description: Free service of the National Council on Aging that connects older adults with benefits programs they may qualify for.

VA Benefits Explorer
Website: www.va.gov/health-care/about-va-health-benefits/long-term-care
Description: Tool to help veterans, service members, and their families find VA benefits they may be eligible to receive.

Caring.com Senior Living Directory
Website: www.caring.com
Description: Searchable database of senior living options including assisted living, memory care, and nursing homes.

Books and Publications

"The 36-Hour Day: A Family Guide to Caring for People Who Have Alzheimer's Disease, Related Dementias, and Memory Loss"
Authors: Nancy L. Mace and Peter V. Rabins
Description: Comprehensive guide for families caring for people with dementia.

"How to Care for Aging Parents"

Author: Virginia Morris

Description: Comprehensive guide covering all aspects of elder care.

"Being Mortal: Medicine and What Matters in the End"

Author: Atul Gawande

Description: Explores the challenges of aging and dying in modern society and how medicine can improve quality of life.

"The Caregiver's Survival Handbook"

Author: Alexis Abramson

Description: Practical guide for managing the emotional and physical challenges of caregiving.

"Get It Together: Organize Your Records So Your Family Won't Have To"

Authors: Melanie Cullen and Shae Irving

Description: Guide to organizing important documents and information for family members.

Technology Resources

Care Coordination Apps

- Caring Bridge (www.caringbridge.org)
- Lotsa Helping Hands (www.lotsahelpinghands.com)
- CaringWire (www.caringwire.com)
- CareZone (www.carezone.com)

Medication Management Tools

- Medisafe (www.medisafeapp.com)
- PillPack by Amazon Pharmacy (www.pillpack.com)
- Hero (www.herohealth.com)

Home Monitoring Systems

- Alarm.com Wellness (www.alarm.com/wellness)
- GrandCare Systems (www.grandcare.com)
- Livio AI (www.starkey.com/hearing-aids/technologies/livio-artificial-intelligence-hearing-aids)

Document Storage Solutions

- Everplans (www.everplans.com)
- Docubank (www.docubank.com)
- FidSafe (www.fidsafe.com)

Telehealth Services

- Teladoc (www.teladoc.com)
- Doctor on Demand (www.doctorondemand.com)
- Amwell (www.amwell.com)

Local Resource Directories

Area Agencies on Aging

Website: www.n4a.org

Description: Network of over 600 agencies nationwide that provide information and assistance on services for older adults and their families.

State Health Insurance Assistance Programs (SHIP)

Website: www.shiphelp.org

Description: State-based programs that offer local, personalized counseling on Medicare and other health insurance options.

State Long-Term Care Ombudsman Programs

Website: ltcombudsman.org

Description: Advocates who work to resolve problems related to the health, safety, welfare, and rights of individuals who live in long-term care facilities.

2-1-1 Helpline

Website: www.211.org

Phone: Dial 2-1-1

Description: Free, confidential service that helps people across North America find local resources they need, including aging.

ENDNOTES

1   Administration for Community Living. LTC: How Much Care Will You Need? https://acl.gov/ltc/basic-needs/how-much-care-will-you-need

2   Centers for Disease Control and Prevention (CDC). National Center for Health Statistics. Life Expectancy. www.cdc.gov/nchs/fastats/life-expectancy.htm

3   Long-term care insurance Facts – Data – Statistics – 2020 Reports: www.aaltci.org/long-term-care-insurance/learning-center/ltcfacts-2020.php

4   Historical population change data (1910-2020): www.census.gov/data/tables/time-series/dec/popchange-data-text.html

5   By 2030, All Baby Boomers will be age 65 or older: www.census.gov/library/stories/2019/12/by-2030-all-baby-boomers-will-be-age-65-or-older.html

6   "Demand for long-term care for services and support will rise": https://www.nasi.org/learn/long-term-services-and-supports/demand-for-long-term-services-and-supports-will-rise

7   AARP & National Alliance for Caregiving, "Caregiving in the U.S. 2020"

8   U.S. Department of Health & Human Services, Administration for Community Living, "How Much Care Will You Need?" https://acl.gov/ltc/basic-needs/how-much-care-will-you-need

9   Ibid

10 Centers for Disease Control and Prevention, "Long-Term Care Providers and Services Users in the United States, 2015–2016," Table 1, www.cdc.gov/nchs/data/series/sr_03/sr03_43-508.pdf

11 American Association for Retired People. (2021). Where we live, where we age: Trends in home and community preferences. https://livablecommunities.aarpinternational.org

12 Administration for Community Living. (2022). 2021 profile of older Americans. https://acl.gov/aging-and-disability-in-america/data-and-research/profile-older-americans

13 Alzheimer's Association, "2024 Alzheimer's Disease Facts and Figures," Alzheimer's & Dementia, Volume 20, Issue 5

14 "Memory care- an in-depth analysis of the sectors standing and dynamics" www.nic.org/blog/memory-care-an-in-depth-analysis-of-the-sectors-standing-and-dynamics/

15   U.S. Department of Health & Human Services, Administration for Community Living, "How Much Care Will You Need?" https://acl.gov/ltc/basic-needs/how-much-care-will-you-need

16   Ibid

17   Ibid

18   Centers for Disease Control and Prevention, "Long-Term Care Providers and Services Users in the United States, 2015–2016," Table 1, www.cdc.gov/nchs/data/series/sr_03/sr03_43-508.pdf

19   www.usaging.org/Files/Senate%20HELP%20Workforce%20RFI%20USAging%20Response.pdf

20   Genworth, "Cost of Care Survey," 2023, www.genworth.com/aging-and-you/finances/cost-of-care.html

21   National Council on Aging, "80% of older adults face financial insecurity" www.ncoa.org/article/80-percent-of-older-adults-face-financial-insecurity/

22   "Healthy Philanthropy Impacting Health and Well-Being of Family Caregivers" - www.gih.org/views-from-the-field/health-philanthropy-impacting-the-health-and-well-being-of-family-caregivers/

23   Genworth Financial, Inc. and CareScout. (2025). Genworth, Cost of Care Survey 2024, https://assets.carescout.com/x/8fcb50422f/282102.pdf

24   Ibid

25   Ibid

26   Federal Reserve, Survey of Consumer Finances 2022

27   New AARP Report Finds Family Caregivers Provide $600 Billion in Unpaid Care Across US" - www.aarp.org/caregiving/financial-legal/unpaid-caregivers-provide-billions-in-care/

28   AARP, Caregiving in the US July 2025

29   Ibid

30   Physical and Mental Effects of Caregiving, https://pmc.ncbi.nlm.nih.gov/articles/PMC2791523/

31   Nationwide Retirement Institute, "Long-Term Care Survey 2025"

32   www.cms.gov/newsroom/fact-sheets/2026-medicare-parts-b-premiums-deductibles

33   Washington Post, "Where do American's live after 85? Look inside the homes of 11 seniors"

34   Caregiver.org, Select Long-Term Statistics

35 Centers for Disease Control and Prevention, "Long-Term Care
    Providers and Services Users in the United States, 2015–2016," Table 1,
    www.cdc.gov/nchs/data/series/sr_03/sr03_43-508.pdf

36 ASPE, Impact of Family and Informal Caregiving to Our Nation:
    https://aspe.hhs.gov/frequently-asked-questions-family-caregiving

37 The MetLife Caregiving Cost Study: Productivity Losses to U.S.
    Business, July 2006

38 American Association for Long-Term Care Insurance (AALTCI),
    Long-Term Care Insurance Facts (2023): "Applicants Declined for
    Health Reasons by Age" (data year 2021). Approvals derived as 100%
    – decline rate. AALTCI Learning Center: www.aaltci.org/long-term-
    care-insurance/learning-center

39 Rowe, J.W., & Kahn, R.L., "Successful Aging," The Gerontologist, 2019

40 Britt, S. (2022). "Self-Assuring: A Middle Path for Long-Term Care
    Planning." Nationwide White Paper

41 "Many Americans are counting on the wrong safety net for long-term
    care" June 16, 2025 - https://news.nationwide.com/many-americans-
    are-counting-on-the-wrong-safety-net-for-long-term-care/

42 Medicare.gov. "What's not covered by Part A & Part B?"

43 www.medicare.gov/coverage/skilled-nursing-facility-care

44 Medicare.gov. "Long-term care"

45 "How long is the average nursing home stay? What to know as you
    plan for care" -www.care.com/c/average-nursing-home-stay/

46 Kaiser Family Foundation. "Medicare Advantage Plans Offering
    Supplemental Benefits: Trends and Implications," 2023

47 Medicare.gov. "What's Medicare Supplement Insurance (Medigap)?"

48 Medicaid.gov, "Spousal Impoverishment Standards," 2024

49 Medicaid.gov, "Medicaid Eligibility: Asset Transfer Rules"

50 Medicaid.gov, "Home & Community-Based Services 1915(c)"

51 "A look at Medicaid waiting list for home and community-based
    services from 2016-2024" - www.kff.org/medicaid/issue-brief/a-look-
    at-waiting-lists-for-medicaid-home-and-community-based-services-
    from-2016-to-2024/

52 Medicaid.gov, "Estate Recovery"

53 U.S. Department of Veterans Affairs, "Aid & Attendance and
    Housebound Benefits," 2024

54 "2025 aid and attendance benefit rates" - https://americanveteransaid.
    com/newblog/2025-aid-and-attendance-benefit-rates/

55 National Pace Association - www.npaonline.org/eligibility-requirements

56 National Pace Association - www.npaonline.org/

57 www.irs.gov/pub/irs-drop/rr-07-13.pdf

58 www.irs.gov/pub/irs-wd/0919011.pdf

59 U.S. Department of Health and Human Services, "How Much Care Will You Need?" LongTermCare.gov, 2023

60 Ibid

61 www.irs.gov/pub/irs-pdf/p502.pdf

62 Ibid

63 www.irs.gov/faqs/interest-dividends-other-types-of-income/life-insurance-disability-insurance-proceeds

64 Ibid

65 Source: U.S. Department of Health and Human Services, Administration for Community Living: How Much Care Will You Need? | LongTermCare.gov

66 Alzheimer's in the Family - www.health.harvard.edu/mind-and-mood/alzheimers-in-the-family

67 "Exploring risks and protective factors in Parkinson's disease" - https://pmc.ncbi.nlm.nih.gov/articles/PMC12110598/

68 Centers for Disease Control and Prevention. "The State of Aging and Health in America 2013"

69 "Caregiving in the United States" - www.aarp.org/content/dam/aarp/ppi/2020/05/full-report-caregiving-in-the-united-states.doi.10.26419-2Fppi.00103.001.pdf

70 Internal Revenue Code (IRC) Section 7702B

71 IRC Section 213(a)

72 IRS Revenue Procedure 2024-38

73 "Enhancing American Retirement Now Act" www.congress.gov/committee-report/117th-congress/senate-report/142/1?outputFormat=pdf

74 Internal Revenue Code (IRC) Section 7702B

75 www.irs.gov/pub/irs-drop/rp-25-32.pdf

76 www.congress.gov/crs_external_products/R/PDF/R45277/R45277.10.pdf

77 www.irs.gov/pub/irs-prior/p969--2024.pdf

78 Ibid

Endnotes

79 Ibid

80 www.irs.gov/pub/irs-drop/n-11-68.pdf

81 Ibid

82 www.irs.gov/pub/irs-regs/td8792.pdf

83 www.irs.gov/pub/irs-prior/p535--2022.pdf

84 www.securian.com/content/dam/doc/il/consumer-tax-reference-ltc-policies-offered-as-an-employee-benefit_87549-109.pdf

85 IRC Section 106 and IRC Section 7702B

86 Internal Revenue Code (IRC) Section 162(l)

87 www.irs.gov/businesses/small-businesses-self-employed/employee-benefits

88 IRC Section 162(l) and IRC Section 213(d)(10)

89 Internal Revenue Code Section 162

90 Ibid

91 Medicaid Planning Assistance, "Estate Planning for Medicaid," published January 20, 2025, by the American Council on Aging www.medicaidplanningassistance.org/estate-planning/

92 National POLST, "What is POLST?" polst.org

93 National Academy of Elder Law Attorneys (NAELA), "Guardianship and Conservatorship: Frequently Asked Questions," naela.org

94 National Academy of Elder Law Attorneys, "Understanding Trusts," naela.org

95 National Academy of Elder Law Attorneys, "Medicaid Planning Strategies," naela.org

96 National Academy of Elder Law Attorneys, "Special Needs Trusts," naela.org

97 Medicaid.gov, "Spousal Impoverishment," medicaid.gov

98 www.oneamerica.com/individuals/offerings/ltc/life-insurance

99 www.nglic.com/ArticleDetails/ArtMID/2221/ArticleID/329/NGL-Launches-New-Long-Term-Care-Insurance-Policyholder-Portal

100 Social Security Administration, "Survivor Benefits," ssa.gov

101 American Association of Long-Term Care Insurance, "Hybrid Long-Term Care Insurance," aaltci.org

102 Social Security Administration, "The Economic Consequences of a Husband's Death: Evidence from the HRS and AHEAD," ssa.gov

103 National Institute on Aging, "Long-Term Care," nia.nih.gov

104 National Alliance for Caregiving and AARP, "Caregiving in the U.S. 2020," May 2020, caregiving.org

105 Administration for Community Living, "2023 Profile of Older Americans," U.S. Department of Health and Human Services, May 2024, acl.gov

106 National Institute on Aging, "Getting Your Affairs in Order," March 2024, nia.nih.gov

107 https://agingsolutions.com/elderly-care-managers-advocate-for-older-adults-and-their-caregivers/

108 Childs, Stephanie. "Solo Agers: Attitudes and Experiences." AARP Research, April 2023, https://doi.org/10.26419/res.00602.001

109 National Council on Aging, "Get the Facts on Economic Security for Seniors," ncoa.org, May 31, 2024, www.ncoa.org/article/get-the-facts-on-economic-security-for-seniors

110 National Association of Insurance Commissioners, "A Shopper's Guide to Long-Term Care Insurance," naic.org

111 American Association for Long-Term Care Insurance, "Long-Term Care Need Statistics for Men and Women," aaltci.org, www.aaltci.org/long-term-care-need/

112 26 U.S.C. §§106, 162(a) (2024); Internal Revenue Service, "Publication 535: Business Expenses," irs.gov, 2024, www.irs.gov/publications/p535.

113 Internal Revenue Service, "Publication 502: Medical and Dental Expenses," irs.gov, 2024, www.irs.gov/publications/p502; Internal Revenue Service, "Publication 15-B: Employer's Tax Guide to Fringe Benefits," irs.gov, 2024, www.irs.gov/publications/p15b

114 Internal Revenue Service, "Publication 535: Business Expenses," irs.gov, 2024, www.irs.gov/publications/p535; Internal Revenue Service, "Publication 525: Taxable and Nontaxable Income," irs.gov, 2024, www.irs.gov/publications/p525

115 Internal Revenue Service, "Publication 502: Medical and Dental Expenses," irs.gov, 2024, www.irs.gov/publications/p502; Internal Revenue Service, "Publication 15-B: Employer's Tax Guide to Fringe Benefits," irs.gov, 2024, www.irs.gov/publications/p15b

116 Internal Revenue Service, "Publication 535: Business Expenses," irs.gov, 2024, www.irs.gov/publications/p535; Internal Revenue Service, "Publication 525: Taxable and Nontaxable Income," irs.gov, 2024, www.irs.gov/publications/p525

117 Internal Revenue Service, "Publication 502: Medical and Dental Expenses," irs.gov, 2024, www.irs.gov/publications/p502; Internal Revenue Service, "Publication 15-B: Employer's Tax Guide to Fringe Benefits," irs.gov, 2024, www.irs.gov/publications/p15b

118 www.aaltci.org/news/long-term-care-insurance-association-news/2025-tax-deductible-limits-long-term-care-insurance

119 IRS Publication 502 (2024) at www.irs.gov/pub/irs-pdf/p502.pdf

120 IRS Publication 525, Taxable and Nontaxable Income (2024), www.irs.gov/pub/irs-pdf/p525.pdf

121 Internal Revenue Service, "Publication 969: Health Savings Accounts and Other Tax-Favored Health Plans," 2024, www.irs.gov/pub/irs-pdf/p969.pdf

122 Versta Research, "2023 LTC Marketing and Thought Leadership Research, Findings from Surveys of Advisors and Consumers," August 2023. https://visit.lfg.com/MG-LTC-PPT004. For a printed copy, call 877-ASK-LINCOLN

123 "Alzheimer's in extended family members increase risk of disease, study shows" www.nia.nih.gov/news/alzheimers-extended-family-members-increased-risk-disease-study-shows

124 Genworth Financial, Inc. (2024). Genworth Cost of Care Survey 2023: Twenty Years of Tracking Long-Term Care Costs. www.genworth.com/aging-and-you/finances/cost-of-care.html

125 Genworth Financial, Inc. and CareScout. (2025). Genworth, Cost of Care Survey 2024, https://assets.carescout.com/x/8fcb50422f/282102.pdf

126 "What is memory care and how much should it cost?" www.assistedliving.org/memory-care/

127 www.morningstar.com/retirement/how-much-should-you-budget-long-term-care July 21st, 2025

DISCLOSURES, DISCLAIMERS, AND LEGAL NOTICES

Please read these notices carefully. They govern your use of this book.

Copyright © 2026 by Amplify FA Inc. All rights reserved. Published by Amplify FA Inc.

Reader Acknowledgment and Agreement

By reading, purchasing, downloading, or using this book in any form, you acknowledge and agree that: (a) this book is provided for general educational purposes only; (b) no professional, advisory, fiduciary, or client relationship of any kind is formed between you and the author or publisher by reason of reading or using this book; (c) you will not rely on any content in this book as a substitute for individualized professional advice from a licensed attorney, tax professional, financial advisor, insurance professional, or healthcare provider; and (d) you accept all limitations of liability described in these notices. If you do not agree to these terms, do not read or use this book.

Insurance Licensing and Jurisdictional Scope

The author, Zach Ott, currently holds the CLTC® designation and a California Resident Insurance Producer License #0E40188 as of the date of publication. As of the date of publication, the author is employed in a wholesale capacity with a financial services firm and is not accepting retail insurance clients. Current employment status, firm affiliations, states of licensure, and professional designations are maintained at www.yourretirementblindspot. com/disclosures and are updated as changes occur.

This book is distributed nationally for general educational purposes only and does not constitute a solicitation, offer, or inducement to purchase any insurance or financial product in any jurisdiction. The mere availability or purchase of this book in a given state does not establish any business relationship, licensed activity, or regulatory presence by the author in that state. Insurance services, consultations, and product recommendations are offered only in jurisdictions where the author holds a current, active license at the time of the engagement.

Readers located in jurisdictions where the author is not currently licensed should not interpret any content in this book as an offer to sell insurance, a solicitation, or insurance advice of any kind. Such readers should consult a locally licensed insurance professional for guidance applicable in their jurisdiction.

Employment, speaking engagements, or future affiliations with insurers or agencies do not change the educational nature of this book and do not constitute endorsements of any product, carrier, or strategy discussed herein.

Educational Purpose Only — No Client or Advisory Relationship

This book provides general educational information about long-term care planning and related financial considerations. It is not individualized advice and does not create a client, advisory, fiduciary, or professional relationship of any kind.

Any professional relationship between the author and a reader must be established through a separate, written engagement agreement signed by both parties. No duty of care, fiduciary duty, or professional obligation of any kind arises from reading this book or from any communication initiated as a result of reading it, unless and until such a written agreement is executed. Before making any planning, financial, insurance, tax, legal, or health-care decisions, consult qualified professionals who can evaluate your specific circumstances.

No Legal, Tax, Investment, Securities, or Medical Advice

The author and publisher are not providing legal, tax, investment, securities, or medical advice through this book. Nothing in this book should be construed as investment advice under the Investment Advisers Act of 1940 or any applicable state or federal securities law. This book does not constitute an offer or solicitation to buy or sell any security, annuity with securities components, insurance product, or financial instrument of any kind.

Laws, regulations, program rules, tax codes, and product features vary significantly by jurisdiction and change over time. Readers should independently verify all information before acting and consult appropriately licensed and qualified professionals.

Accuracy and Time Sensitivity

Information in this book is believed to be accurate as of December 2025 but may have changed and may contain errors or omissions. Verify current terms, costs, product features, benefit rules, and applicable regulations before taking any action. Where data, rules, or product details are referenced, readers should confirm current information with primary sources or product carriers.

Products, Carriers, and Illustrations

References to products, carriers, or programs are for illustration only and do not constitute recommendations, endorsements, offers, or guarantees. Any examples or illustrations, including hybrid long-term care examples, reflect assumptions as of the date noted and are not quotes, contracts, or guarantees of any kind.

Features, rider availability, benefits, and costs vary by age, health, underwriting classification, product, carrier, and state of issue; riders may involve additional charges and limitations. Guarantees are subject to the claims-paying ability of the issuing insurance company. Tax treatment of any product or benefit depends on individual facts and circumstances; consult a qualified tax professional before acting.

"Navigator Stories" — Hypothetical Scenarios

Case studies and "Navigator Stories" in this book are hypothetical or anonymized composite scenarios created solely for educational illustration. They do not depict actual persons, events, or outcomes, and do not predict, promise, or guarantee any result. Details may be changed or omitted to protect privacy. Results vary based on individual circumstances, health, underwriting, product features, state law, and future changes in rules and pricing.

No reader may rely on any hypothetical scenario, case study, or Navigator Story as the basis for any legal claim, regulatory complaint, arbitration demand, or grievance of any kind against the author or publisher.

Tax Content — General Education Only

Tax information in this book is general education only and does not constitute tax advice. Federal and state tax laws, regulations, and administrative guidance change frequently and apply differently based on individual facts and circumstances. Readers should consult a qualified tax professional (CPA, EA, or tax attorney) before taking any action.

Tax summaries, thresholds, and examples are simplified and based on sources believed reliable as of December 2025. Examples may omit exceptions or special rules and are not guarantees of outcomes. Readers should independently verify current law, thresholds, inflation adjustments, and administrative guidance before acting.

Sources, Citations, and Precedential Value

Where possible, citations reference primary sources (Internal Revenue Code, Treasury Regulations, IRS Publications and Forms, Revenue Rulings/Procedures, Notices, and official agency guidance). IRS Private Letter Rulings (PLRs) and Chief Counsel Advice, if mentioned, are not precedential authority and may not be relied upon by taxpayers other than the original requester. State and local rules vary; references to California law or Medi-Cal are state-specific and may not apply elsewhere.

Citations and Links

Every effort has been made to cite accurate, reliable sources. Web pages change over time and links can become unavailable. If a link is unavailable, search by title or citation, visit the issuing agency's website directly, or use an archived copy (e.g., the Internet Archive/Wayback Machine). Citations were current as of December 2025. Corrections may be submitted to info@ yourretirementblindspot.com and will be posted at www.your-retirementblindspot.com/updates. The author and publisher are not responsible for third-party changes or dead links.

No Penalty Protection (Circular 230 Notice)

No portion of this material is intended or written to be used, and cannot be used, by any taxpayer for the purpose of avoiding penalties that may be imposed under the Internal Revenue Code or applicable state law.

Government Non-Endorsement

The author is not affiliated with, connected to, or endorsed by the U.S. government, any federal agency, any state government, or any state agency, including Medicare, Medi-Cal, Medicaid, or the Social Security Administration. No government program endorses this book or any recommendation herein.

Limitation of Liability and Disclaimer of Warranties

To the fullest extent permitted by applicable law, the author and publisher disclaim all warranties, express or implied, including but not limited to implied warranties of merchantability, fitness for a particular purpose, accuracy, and non-infringement, and shall not be liable for any losses or damages of any kind, including without limitation direct, indirect, incidental, consequential, punitive, or special damages, arising out of or in connection with the use of or reliance on this book or its contents.

Nothing in this disclaimer limits the author's or publisher's liability for gross negligence, willful misconduct, or fraud. To the fullest extent permitted by applicable law, in no event shall the total aggregate liability of the author or publisher to any reader or third party exceed the actual purchase price paid by that reader for this book.

No Guarantees or Promises

This book does not guarantee results, eligibility for benefits, or specific financial, medical, insurance, or tax outcomes of any kind. Any opinions expressed are solely the author's personal views and are not guarantees of performance or outcomes. Past examples, illustrations, or scenarios do not guarantee similar future results.

Trademarks

CLTC® and Certified in Long-Term Care® are registered trademarks of Certification for Long-Term Care, LLC. The author currently holds the CLTC® designation as of the date of publication. Current designation status is maintained at www.yourretirementblindspot.com/disclosures. Readers may independently verify the author's current CLTC® designation status at the official registry: www.ltc-cltc.com/cltc/findCLTC. Use of the CLTC® designation does not imply that Certification for Long-Term Care, LLC has reviewed, endorsed, or approved this book. All other trademarks, service marks, and trade names referenced herein remain the property of their respective owners; use does not imply affiliation, sponsorship, or endorsement.

Consultations, Suitability, and Subsequent Engagements

The author is not currently accepting individual consultations or retail insurance engagements. Readers seeking personalized insurance or financial planning guidance should consult a qualified licensed professional in their jurisdiction.

Severability

If any provision of this disclaimer is held to be invalid, illegal, or unenforceable in any jurisdiction, such invalidity or unenforceability shall not affect any other provision or render this disclaimer unenforceable in any other jurisdiction. The remaining provisions shall continue in full force and effect to the maximum extent permitted by law.

Governing Law and Dispute Resolution

This disclaimer and any dispute, claim, or controversy arising out of or related to this book, its contents, or the author's educational activities shall be governed by and construed in accordance with the laws of the State of California, without regard to its conflict of laws principles. Any legal action or proceeding must be brought exclusively in the state or federal courts located in the State of California, and each reader, by using this book, consents to the exclusive personal jurisdiction of those courts.

Updates and Errata

Tax thresholds, regulatory rules, insurance product features, and program eligibility criteria change over time. For updates and corrections, visit: www.yourretirementblindspot.com/updates. Tax content and product information last reviewed December 2025.